CHILDREN OF POVERTY

STUDIES ON THE EFFECTS OF SINGLE PARENTHOOD, THE FEMINIZATION OF POVERTY, AND HOMELESSNESS

edited by

STUART BRUCHEY
ALLAN NEVINS PROFESSOR EMERITUS
COLUMBIA UNIVERSTIY

A ROUTLEDGE SERIES

HOMELESSNESS AND ITS CONSEQUENCES

THE IMPACT ON CHILDREN'S PSYCHOLOGICAL WELL-BEING

Rosemarie Theresa Downer

ROUTLEDGE
NEW YORK & LONDON

Published in 2001 by
Routledge
29 West 35th Street
New York, NY 10001

Published in Great Britain by
Routledge
11 New Fetter Lane
London EC4P 4EE

Routledge is an imprint of the Taylor & Francis Group.
Copyright © 2001 by Rosemarie T. Downer

All rights reserved. No part of this book may be reprinted or reproduced or utilized in any form or by any electronic, mechanical, or other means, now known or hereafter invented, including photocopying and recording, or in any information storage or retrieval system, without written permission from the publishers.

10 9 8 7 6 5 4 3 2 1

Library of Congress Cataloging-in-Publication Data

Downer, Rosemarie Theresa, 1959–
  Homelessness and its consequences: the impact on children's psychological well-being / by Rosemarie Theresa Downer.
    p. cm.
  Includes bibliographocal references and index.
  ISBN 0-8153-3580-6
  1. Homeless children—United States—Psychology. 2. Homeless families—United States. 3. Child psychology—United States. I. Title.

HV4505 .D68 2001
362.7'086'942—dc21

2001041601

Printed on acid-free, 250 year-life paper
Manufactured in the United States of America

To my dear Mom and my friend Lisa who have stuck with me through good times and bad. And to Rod and Rachel who have given me countless hours of computer consultation.

Contents

Foreword	xi
Preface	xiii
Introduction	xv
Acknowledgments	xxv
Tables and Figures	xxvii
List of Abbreviations	xxxi
Chapter I: Homelessness-A Historical Perspective	1
Chapter II: Homelessness Today	3
Pathways to Homelessness	4
Chapter III: The Multidimensional Effects of Homelessness	9
Impact of Homelessness on Parents	9
Parenting Stress and Quality	12
Social Support	14
Impact of Homelessness on Children	15
Physical Implications	15
Psychological and Developmental Implications	16
Educational Implications	19
Conclusions	21

Chapter IV: The Formation of Self-concept	23
Parental Influences on Children's Self-concept	24
The Influence of Homelessness on Parent-Child Relationships	25
Parent Self-concept, Family Functioning and their Effects on the Parenting Role and Children's Self-concept	27
Self-concept and its Relation to Behavioral Problems	28
Conclusion	29
Chapter V: Research Design and Methodology	31
Participants	32
Measures	33
Procedures	38
Chapter VI: Results	43
Overview	43
Section I – Characteristics of Homeless and Housed Families	43
Section II – The Functioning of Housed and Homeless Families and Children	46
Family Functioning Variables	46
Child Outcome Variables	48
Family Functioning Variables and Child Outcome Variables	64
Exploratory Analyses	68
Chapter VII: Implications of Findings	77
The Effects of Poverty Coupled with Homelessness on Families	78
Social Support	79
Family Processes	80
Parenting Capacity	82
Behavioral Problems of Homeless and Housed Children	84
Relationships Between Family Functioning Variables and Child Outcome Variables	86
Predictors of Child Well-being	87
Conclusions	89
Policy and Program Implications	90
Limitations of the Study	92
Appendix A Research Summary/Description	95
Appendix B Request for Research Participants	97
Appendix C Consent Form	99

Contents

Appendix D	Standardized Instructions – Before Parent Interviews	101
Appendix E	Standardized Instructions – Before Child Interviews	103
Appendix F	Participant Screening Sheet – Homeless	105
Appendix G	Participant Screening Sheet – Housed	107
Appendix H	Family Support Scale (FSS)	109
Appendix I	Social Embeddedness Questionnaire (SEQ)	111
Appendix J	The Family Environment Scale (FES)	113
Appendix K	Parenting Dimensions Inventory (PDI)	121
Appendix L	Child Behavior Checklist (CBCL)	125
Appendix M	Piers-Harris-Children's Self-concept Scale (CSCS)	129
Appendix N	Qualitative Data – Parents	133
Appendix O	Qualitative Data – Children	135
Bibliography		137
Subject Index		155
Name Index		159

Foreword

Having worked with homeless families as a direct service provider and an administrator for over a decade, I have witnessed the developmental impact of homelessness on all its victims. The inherently negative nature of homelessness makes responding to the needs of the homeless a mammoth task. In addition, the limited perspective that key individuals such as some government officials, policy makers and service providers take on the matter intensifies the challenge.

Homelessness is often viewed as an economic problem – lack of affordable housing and lack of financial resources. Therefore, the response is often to create emergency shelters, transitional housing programs, and housing subsidies, then later move the homeless into permanent housing until they recycle back through the system. Many successful efforts have been made across the country to provide emergency shelter, transitional and affordable permanent housing for homeless families. However, many of these families are unable to maintain housing. In fact, many are unable to maintain shelter by adhering to program rules and regulations under supervision. It is, therefore, increasingly difficult for these families to maintain private housing without supervision. This then results in relatively brief stays in private housing, resulting in high rates of recidivism.

The question is "Why is it that a homeless mother who moved directly from shelter where she lived in a dormitory among strangers with her four children, was required to comply with shelter rules, and had limited autonomy, even over her own children cannot maintain housing when attained?" One would assume that, private housing offers all the securities of life that shelter-living deprives her of — privacy, autonomy, a sense of ownership, a sense of accomplishment, space, independence, etc. To further complicate the question, the housing is affordable ($16 per month) and is newly built and equipped with all new appliances and carpeting. Why can't the mother, the head of household, maintain the house she longed for while in shelter

Foreword

per monthly? Provisions are also made for the mother
'y payment because it was determined based on her
 ..ι other expenses, such as utilities, toiletries, food, trans-
 ..ephone, clothing, and savings were budgeted.
 ..eve the answer is obvious - the problem is not solely a lack of finan-
..αl resources or housing. The problem is more complex than a lack of concrete resources, it is due to inefficient underlying family and individual functioning that lead to poor decision-making and negative life events and outcomes. Homelessness then becomes a negative event for these families, and is only a symptom of existing underlying problems.

I believe that, of all the victims of homelessness, the children suffer to the greatest degree. After being born into an unstable family, to parents who are challenged by providing the basics of life, they are then deprived of a fundamental need, a home, often at a critical time in their development. Therefore, while they face the negative impact of homelessness they are not at liberty to rely on their primary caregivers for support because they themselves are challenged. Children, therefore, are at risk of impaired development in all domains and adverse generational socialization.

While the need for affordable housing is not denied, this book high-lights the psychological impact of homelessness on parent-child relationships, family functioning, and children's psychological well-being. Recommendations are also made for program design and implementation and policy development.

Preface

Homelessness is an ever-growing social challenge that has a negative impact on all its victims, particularly the children. In order for children to grow up to be functioning and contributing members of society, they must develop adequate cognitive, physical and psychosocial skills. Homeless children, who are the focus of this work, are deprived of the basic experiences that foster healthy development.

There are numerous pathways into homelessness; thus homeless individuals are not a monolithic and homogenous population. Some factors that contribute to the different pathways into homelessness include lack of affordable housing, domestic violence, eviction, substance abuse, financial instability, natural causes such as floods and fires, unemployment, family discord, and generational poverty (Weitzman et al., 1990). In addition to these negative experiences, homeless parents usually have limited education (Bassuk and Rosenberg, 1988; Bassuk, Rubin and Lauriat, 1986) and minimal social support (Zeisemer, Marcoux and Marwell, 1994) from family and friends. These problems present some immediate challenges for parents who need emotional support before they can address the emotional needs of their children. Even more fundamentally, homeless parents wake up daily to the continuing problem of meeting their children's basic need for food and shelter. This engenders feelings of inadequacy, poor self-efficacy in the areas of parenting and being a provider, and additional distraction from the parenting role.

As a consequence of these factors, homeless children are at risk for physical, cognitive, and psychosocial deprivation. However, there is relatively little empirical research that examines whether homeless children do experience compromised psychological well-being relative to their housed peers.

Clinical and empirical research has pointed to the key role of parents in the development of children, particularly their self-concept (Bronfenbrenner, 1986, Coopersmith, 1967; Goodman, Adamson, Riniti,

Preface

'leen, 1993; Sullivan, 1945). However, homeless parents ⟩ggle to meet their own emotional needs, sometimes at ⌐hildren's needs.

⟩ ↩hen becomes daily survival rather than long range planning ⌐ɪɪld care, schooling, and employment. Even long-term affordable ⌐sıng is not highly prioritized (Ziefert and Strauch-Brown, 1991). This document is written from the perspective that children's self-concept is a product of a sense of successive comparisons and contrasts between self, father, and mother (Lifshitz, 1975) and that parental support, nurturance, and emotional availability influence the children's self-concept most (Goodman et al., 1994; Killeen, 1993). If the parents are unsuccessful at providing for their children and if they are preoccupied with meeting the basic needs of their families, there is a strong likelihood that the parents will not provide favorable models with which the children should compare themselves, and they will be less emotionally available and less nurturing to their children. Also, it is very unlikely that the children of the target population of this study will have fathers with which to compare themselves (Homes for the Homeless, 1992). Therefore these children will have one less significant figure with whom to make successive comparisons and contrasts.

This work explored how process resources, such as social support, interpersonal relationships, personal growth; and parenting quality of homeless and housed families relate to the children's psychological well-being (See Figure 1). Process resources are defined as emotional supports within the family, particularly those available from the parents to the children. Such resources include social support, interpersonal relationships, personal growth, and parenting quality. Psychological well-being was measured using two variables; (1) self-concept and (2) behavioral problems. Two types of families were included in the study — currently homeless and a comparison group of housed low-income families.

Introduction

Although many children of the United States grow up healthy and happy in strong, stable families, far too many do not. Today, children comprise the poorest group in the United States and America's youngest children are more likely to live in poverty than Americans in any other age group. During the past two decades, there has been a substantial increase in the number and percentage of poor young children in the United States. The child poverty rate has grown among all racial and ethnic groups, and in urban, suburban, and rural areas. One in five children lives in a family with income below the federal poverty level. In 1998, 19% of all children under 18 years of age lived below the federal poverty level (U.S. Census Bureau, 1999). In 1996, nine percent of children lived in extreme poverty, that is, with an income below 50% of the federal poverty level (U.S. Department of Commerce, Bureau of Census, 1989, p.7, Kids Count, 1999). One in four infants and toddlers under the age of three is poor. Nearly 13 million children live in poverty, many of which are extremely poor, over two million more than a decade ago (U.S. Department of Commerce, Bureau of Census, 1990).

According to the National Commission for Children (1991), impoverished children often have parents who are too stressed and too busy to provide caring, attention and guidance. The children sometimes grow up without the material and emotional support of their parents. They may be raised in homes permeated with violence or substance abuse. Often their families cannot adequately feed or clothe them nor provide safe, secure homes. A disproportionate number of these children are victims of abuse and neglect at the hands of adults they love and trust, as well as those they do not even know. They have higher rates of prematurity, low birth weight, and chronic physical morbidity (National Commission on Children, 1991). Many of these children enter schools ill prepared for rigorous learning and fail to develop the skills and attitudes needed to get good jobs (National

Commission for Children, 1991). There is substantial evidence that poor children have poorer self-concept (Bruner, 1975) and are exposed to more impaired family and marital relationships (Conger, Lorenz and Elder, 1992; McLoyd, 1990) than more affluent families. One of the most disadvantaged group of families is homeless families residing in shelters and motels.

Homelessness is a multifaceted phenomenon that deprives its victims of a stable, nurturing environment. The most helpless of this victimized population, the children, experience this loss at a time in their lives when the absence of stable, nurturing settings is most injurious—when they are developing a sense of themselves, a sense of their own self-worth and their own capabilities (Rivlin, 1990).

All personal experiences are intrinsically connected to their particular place of occurrence. The specific features of these places – objects, sounds, people, and ambiance are all unique distinctions that make direct contributions to children's lives; their cognitive, social, and emotional development, and their personalities. The surroundings in which the children are raised and both the minor children and adult occupants of these surroundings help distinguish the children from others and help to define the world in which they live. These environments have the potential to provide children with a sense of security and a sense of belongingness — two main ingredients for the development of a secure sense of self. Children who are born and raised in shelters are moved from one precarious or doubled-up/overcrowded living arrangement to another. They are deprived of the opportunity to make a healthy connection with personalized surroundings and their unique features (Rivlin, 1990).

The reports of the plight of the homeless often refer to homeless adults; therefore, the most helpless victims, the children, may go unnoticed. Homelessness is an extremely costly and disruptive experience for children. It complicates their lives by adversely impacting their physical, cognitive and psychosocial health (Bassuk, 1991; Klein, 1990; Molnar, Rath and; Rafferty and Shinn, 1991; Wagner and Pervine, 1994).

The frequent moves, unpredictable future, less than optimal education for the children, and the daily struggles of the parents to meet the basic needs of their families are likely to have negative effects on all involved. In particular, homelessness can be expected to have negative effects on the children's psychological well-being. Scientific research has shown that parents play a key role in the development of their children's self-concept (Killeen, 1993; Lifshitz, 1975). Due to the daily struggles associated with homelessness, parents are likely to be less emotionally available to their children. This may have a negative impact on children's development of a healthy self-concept.

Process resources are defined as emotional supports that are found within the family. In contrast to process resources, structural resources are defined as material support within the family or as the structure of the family, namely; parent composition, family income, and family size. Research has examined the relation between children's self-concept and the family's structural resources such as family structure (Beer, 1989; Kurtz, 1994; McCullough, Ashbridge, and Pegg, 1994) and income level of parents (Killeen, 1993).

Family structure and income are related to children's self-concept during the adolescent years. McCullough et al. (1994) found that of two groups of adolescents, those from single parent households had lower self-esteem.

Despite existing research that examine the relationship between family structure and children's self-concept, there has been very little study of how family process resources such as social support, family relationships, and personal growth within the family impact children's psychological well-being.

Although homelessness appears to have deleterious effects on its victims, much of the earlier research has been limited to the assessment of the number and characteristics of the homeless. However, more sophisticated studies utilizing longitudinal and ethnographic methods are now being conducted (Blasi, 1990). But to date, not enough attention has been given to homelessness and its effects on children's psychological well-being. While it is well documented that other forms of family dysfunction such as substance abuse, domestic violence, and divorce negatively affect the offsprings' self-concept (Amato, 1986; Bishop and Ingersol, 1989). There is a pronounced paucity of research about the psychosocial effects of homelessness, on children.

Most policy makers and service providers view homelessness as a solely economic phenomenon while they ignore the clinical bases and effects of this negative life experience. While acknowledging that economics does play a part in homelessness, this work examined the effects of homelessness on children's psychological well-being, their self-concept and behavioral problems.

In researching the effects of homelessness, it is important to establish a low-income comparison group, and so, housed low-income families with children served as the comparison group. There is a body of research that reports that poverty has negative effects on the parent-child relationship (McLoyd, 1990; Pelton, 1981; Newberger, Hampton, Marx, and White, 1986; Oates, 1986; Straus, 1980; Whipple and Webster, 1991). Homelessness is an expression of extreme poverty, but one can be poor and not be homeless. The effects of homelessness may be best understood from a micro level, rather than a macrolevel of poverty in general. Therefore, an examination of whether or not homeless and housed families look different in the area of family process resources will begin to explain whether or not the added stress of homelessness has an effect over and above poverty on the children's psychological well-being.

The findings of this study shed some light on the possible psychosocial effects of homelessness. The study compares the process resources of homeless and housed low-income families, clarifying areas of similarity and dissimilarity

Hypotheses

(1) Homeless families have less informal support, formal support, perceived support, and social embeddedness than housed low-income families.

(2) Homeless families have poorer interpersonal relationships than housed low-income families.

(3) Homeless families reflect less personal growth than housed low-income families.

(4) Homeless parents have poorer parenting quality than housed low-income parents.

(5) Homeless children have poorer self-concept than housed low-income children.

(6) Homeless children have more behavioral problems than housed low-income children.

(7) There are positive correlations among family process resources, such as personal growth, interpersonal relationships, and parenting quality, and children's self-concept within both groups of families.

(8) There are negative correlations among family process resources, such as parenting quality, interpersonal relationships, and personal growth, and children's behavioral problems within both groups of families.

Definition of Terms
General Concepts

(1) Homeless - The state of having to sleep in a public facility due to the lack of a private/personal dwelling place.

(2) Low-income - Recipients of Aid to Families with Dependent Children (AFDC), now known as Temporary Assistance to Needy Families (TANF) and Head Start and/or lunch program participant.

(3) Self-concept - The global and domain specific feelings about or perceptions of the self, including behavior, intellect and school status, physical appearance and attributes, anxiety, popularity, and happiness and satisfaction.

(4) Stress - No consistent definition of stress has been utilized in the literature and the distinction between stress and stressor is often overlooked. Stressors are life events, hassles, transitions and related hardships that produce tensions that call for management. When this tension is not overcome, stress emerges. Stress has been defined as the product of the interaction of

the subjectively defined demands of a situation and the capacity of an individual to respond to these demands (Straus, 1980).

Concepts Measured

(1) Process Resources - Emotional support within the family, particularly those available from the parents to the children. The process resources that are measured are social support (enacted-formal and informal, social embeddedness, and perceived support), interpersonal relationships, personal growth, and parenting quality.

(i) Social Support - Social support is generally defined as "an individual's belief that s/he is cared for, esteemed, and has people to turn to in times of need" (Koblinsky and Anderson, 1993a, p.2) or a network of free and intangible assistance available from friends and family. Informal support is a feeling of care and esteem from family, friends, co-workers, spouse, and social groups. Formal support is assistance received from professional sources such as social service agencies, teachers and doctors. Enacted support is a combination of formal and informal support. Perceived support is a measure of the amount of informal support available, and social embeddedness is a measure of the consistency or stability of the perceived informal support. Informal and formal support are measured by the Family Support Scale (FSS) (Dunst, Jenkins, and Trivette, 1984), and perceived support and social embeddedness are measured by the *Social Embeddedness Questionnaire* (SEQ) (Letiecq, Anderson, and Koblinsky, 1996)

(ii) Interpersonal Relationship - A family functioning variable that measures cohesion, expressiveness, and conflict within the families.

(iii) Personal Growth - A family functioning variable that measures independence, achievement orientation, intellectual cultural orientation, active recreational orientation, and moral religious emphasis. Interpersonal relationships and personal growth are measured by the *Family Environment Scale* (FES) (Moos and Moos, 1981).

(iv) Parenting Quality, - Defined by parental support, parental structure, and parental control. Parental support assesses nurturing and accepting behaviors with children, and responsiveness to children. Parental structure assesses consistency and organization in the parent-child relationship, and parental control assesses the amount of control and maturity demands exercised by the parents. Parenting quality is measured by the use of the *Parenting_Dimensions Inventory* (PDI) (Power, 1989).

(3) Behavioral Problems - Children's, internal and external, socially unacceptable behaviors across time and situations. Internal behaviors are behaviors that are not directed toward others but are directed toward the self. External behaviors are those that are directed to others. Both internal and external behaviors are measured by the *Child Behavior Checklist* (CBCL) (Achenbach and Edelbrock, 1983).

(4) Self-concept - The children's perceptions about the self in the areas of behavior, intellectual and social status, physical appearance, anxiety, popularity, happiness and satisfaction, and global self-concept. A low score in any of these domains reflect a low self-concept. Specific domains and global self-concept is measured by the *Piers-Harris Children's Self-concept Scale (CSCS) (The Way I Feel About Myself)* (Piers and Harris, 1969).

Theoretical Bases of the Study
The theoretical bases upon which this research is built are the following: (1) Maslow's (1954) theory of the hierarchy of needs; (2) Markus, Crane, Bernstein, and Siladi's (1982) theory of social experiences, cognitive structures and resulting self-concept; and (3) Sullivan's (1945) theory of children's self-concept development.

Maslow (1954) constructed a hierarchy of needs, ascending from the basic physiological needs to the more complex psychological motives that become important only after the needs at the lower levels have been at least partially satisfied before those at the higher levels become important determinants of action.

Maslow's (1954) theory is selected as a support for this study because homeless families' basic physiological needs, those that are at the bottom of the hierarchy of needs are not adequately met. These are physiological needs of food and shelter. The second level of needs is for safety, order, security, and stability. According to Maslow, if the needs at the lower levels are not adequately met then the individual will not be motivated to meet the needs at the more complex psychological levels.

Some of the more complex psychological needs are for belongingness and love, and the need for self-esteem, respect, and success. Therefore, according to Maslow (1954), because homeless families' basic physiological needs are not being met, there is reason to believe that their more complex psychological needs are also unmet. Since the needs at the lower levels must be at least partially satisfied first, it is believed that homeless parents will be more occupied with the demands of the lower levels, resulting in a neglect of those at the higher levels.

Parenting and the fostering of a healthy psychological well-being in children require attention to features of the higher levels — security, stability, love, affection, belongingness, and self-esteem. However, because homeless families are at the lowest level of the hierarchy, it can be speculated that positive parenting and the fostering of a healthy self-concept in homeless children are at risk. See Figure 1.

Markus et al. (1982) postulated that with social experiences we gain a diversity of self-relevant information that becomes organized into cognitive structures. We categorize, explain, and evaluate our behavior in various focal domains according to those cognitive structures. These cognitive structures are referred to as self-schemas, and a combination of these self-schemas in various domains forms the self-concept. See Figure 2.

Figure 1. A Comparison of Maslow's Hierarchy of Needs to the Conditions Experienced by Homeless Families.

General Population	Homeless Population
Self-actualization	Lack of fulfillment
Self-esteem, respect and sucess	Lost autonomy, public parenting, nemployment, failure as a provider.
Belongingness and love	Fragmented families, separation, divorce, lack of social support
Safety, security, order and stability	Multi-residence and multi-schools per year. Residence in motels and shelters. Precarious housing.
Physiological Needs - hunger, thirst, and sex	Physiological Needs - dependence on shelters and soup kitchens

Sullivan (1945) postulated that individuals' self-concept is influenced by how others view them. For Sullivan (1945), social interactions form the basis for self-concept development, with children's comparisons of themselves with others providing normative information about their skills, talents, and interests.

Markus et al. (1982) theory of social experiences, cognitive structures and resulting self-concept and Sullivan's (1945) theory of children's self-concept development are used as theoretical bases of this study because they provide clear explanations of how homeless children's social experiences can contribute to the shaping of their self-concept and how the parents' experiences can influence the children's development.

All the social experiences that the children have, particularly the ones that they have with their parents, will contribute to how they define themselves. If, according to Maslow's theory, the parents are preoccupied with meeting the basic physiological needs of family members then the chances of emotionally enriched and nurturing experiences with the children are limited. Therefore, the children are likely to have less nurturing and emotionally impoverished social experiences with their parents that will negatively affect their psychological well-being.

Figure 2. The Relation Between Social Experiences and Self-schemas to the Resulting Self-concept.

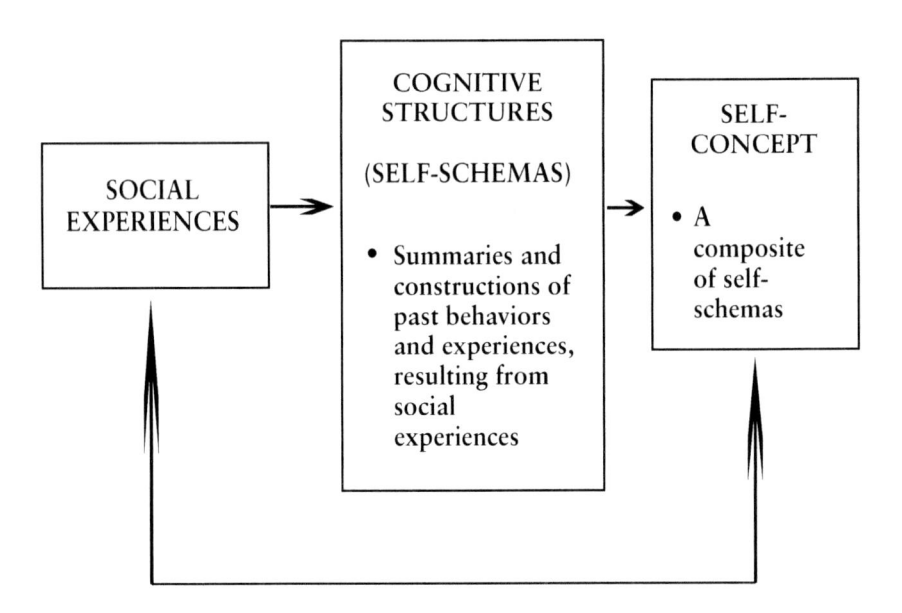

```
┌──────────────┐     ┌────────────────────┐     ┌──────────────┐
│              │     │    COGNITIVE       │     │   SELF-      │
│              │     │    STRUCTURES      │     │   CONCEPT    │
│   SOCIAL     │ ──> │   (SELF-SCHEMAS)   │ ──> │              │
│ EXPERIENCES  │     │                    │     │ • A          │
│              │     │ • Summaries and    │     │   composite  │
│              │     │   constructions of │     │   of self-   │
└──────────────┘     │   past behaviors   │     │   schemas    │
       ▲             │   and experiences, │     └──────────────┘
       │             │   resulting from   │            ▲
       │             │   social           │            │
       │             │   experiences      │            │
       │             └────────────────────┘            │
       └──────────────────────────────────────────────┘
```

Straus' (1980) theory of the defective role that stress plays in the parent-child relationship also adds to the foundation of this study. Homelessness is clearly a stressful experience for all involved. Homeless parents experience ongoing stress around their inability to provide for their children, living within the confines of shelter rules, responding to the demands of their case workers, and parenting under the scrutiny of shelter staff and other professionals almost at all times. In many shelters, "Each and every activity is done in public, that is, the women do their mothering in the company and in full view of others." (Boxill and Beaty, 1987, p.52). These are ongoing stressors that have a high likelihood of negatively affecting the parent-child relationship.

According to Straus (1980), stressors are negative experiences that produce tension that requires management. When this tension is not overcome, stress emerges. Homeless families experience shelter living, and lost autonomy through their responses to the many demands placed on them by their caseworkers, shelter staff and the Social Services system. Such experiences may tax parents' ability to manage their tension, resulting in stress. Therefore, according to Straus (1980), with the existence of stress, the parent-child relationship is likely to be negatively affected, compromising the psychological well-being of the children.

Significance of the Study

To this date, limited research has been conducted that examines the relationship between process resources among homeless families and homeless children's self-concept. In this study, the process resources and family functioning of homeless families are examined which further delineates the strengths and weaknesses of these families and their impact on the children's psychological well-being. This study adds to existing research by comparing the process resources and family functioning of homeless and housed families. The study examines the relationship between process resources and two measures of children's psychological well-being (self-concept and behavioral problems) in the two housing groups.

This study also adds to the discussion of a broader issue — poverty and the developing child, and poverty and parent-child relationships. The issue of stress and the need for social support is also brought into focus. Poverty in general, and more specifically, homelessness are stressful life experiences. Their effects on parents, family functioning, and ultimately the children's psychological well-being are examined.

The findings of this study can be beneficial to policy makers and service providers. In addition, this study highlights the need for further research that looks at homelessness from a microlevel and not from the macrolevel of poverty. It also points to the need for programs that provide services that seek to address and ameliorate the psychosocial impact of the unique experiences of homeless children and parents. Service providers and policy makers are reminded that the response to homelessness is not solely economic, neither is it solely one of affordable housing. This study supports the position that the response to homelessness must be comprehensive, to include economical/physical, emotional/social, and educational services.

Finally, the study makes a contribution to existing literature on the psychological well-being of homeless children, low-income families' process resources and parent-child relationships.

Acknowledgments

This study would not have become a reality had it not been for the assistance offered by a number of individuals. Specific individuals to whom special "thank yous" are extended include Dr. Brenda Jones Harden, Dr. Charles Flatter, Dr. Sally Koblinsky, Dr. Allan Wigfield, and Dr. William Schaffer.

Of equal importance are all the shelter directors and administrators who gave me access to their programs to gather data and all the shelter residents who voluntarily participated in the interviews for data collection.

Finally, I must say thanks to all my family members and friends who provided moral support throughout this tedious process.

Tables and Figures

1. Figure 1 : A Comparison of Maslow's Hierarchy of Needs to the Conditions Experienced by Homeless Families — xxi
2. Figure 2 : The Relation Between Social Experiences and Self-schemas to the Resulting Self-concept — xxii
3. Figure 3 : Analytic Model of how Poverty and Economic Loss Affect Children (McLoyd, 1990) — 10
4. Table 1 : Hypotheses and Corresponding Analytic Plan — 33
5. Figure 4 : Multidimensional Parenting Model (Slater and Power, 1987) — 37
6. Table 2 : Instruments and the Variables Measured by Each One — 40
7. Table 3 : Parent Demographics — 44
8. Table 4 : Frequency Distribution — Child Demographics — 45
9. Table 5 : Mean Ages of Parents and Children — 45
10. Table 6 : Results of Chi Squares Comparing Homeless and Housed Parents — 46
11. Table 7 : Results of Chi Squares Comparing Homeless and Housed Children — 46
12. Table 8 : Comparison of Means Among Family Functioning Variables — 47
13. Table 9 : Ratings of Homeless and Housed Children in Self-concept Domains — 49
14. Table 10 : Ratings of Homeless Boys and Girls in Self-concept Domains — 50
15. Table 11 : Ratings of Housed Boys and Girls in Self-concept Domains — 51
16. Table 12 : Ratings of Homeless and Housed Boys in Behavioral Problems — 52

17. Table 13 : Ratings of Homeless and Housed Girls in Behavioral Problems — 52
18. Table 14 : Chi Squares – Child Outcome Variables — 53
19. Table 15 : 2 x 2 ANOVA Table – Anxiety Self-concept — 54
20. Table 16 : 2-Way ANOVA Table – Anxiety Self-concept — 54
21. Table 17 : 2 x 2 ANOVA Table – Behavior Self-concept — 55
22. Table 18 : 2-Way ANOVA Table – Behavior Self-concept — 55
23. Table 19 : 2 x 2 ANOVA Table – Happiness Self-concept — 56
24. Table 20 : 2-Way ANOVA Table – Happiness Self-concept — 56
25. Table 21 : 2 x 2 ANOVA Table – Intelligence and School Status Self-concept — 57
26. Table 22 : 2-Way ANOVA Table – Intelligence and School Status Self-concept — 57
27. Table 23 : 2 x 2 ANOVA Table – Physical Self-concept — 58
28. Table 24 : 2-Way ANOVA Table – Physical Self-concept — 58
29. Table 25 : 2 x 2 ANOVA Table – Popularity Self-concept — 59
30. Table 26 : 2-Way ANOVA Table – Popularity Self-concept — 59
31. Table 27 : 2 x 2 ANOVA Table – Global Self-concept — 60
32. Table 28 : 2-Way ANOVA Table – Global Self-concept — 60
33. Table 29 : 2 x 2 ANOVA Table – External Behavioral Problems — 61
34. Table 30 : 2-Way ANOVA Table – External Behavioral Problems — 61
35. Table 31 : 2 x 2 ANOVA Table – Internal Behavioral Problems — 62
36. Table 32 : 2-Way ANOVA Table – Internal Behavioral Problems — 62
37. Table 33 : 2 x 2 ANOVA Table – Total Behavioral Problems — 63

38.	Table 34 : 2-Way ANOVA Table – Total Behavioral Problems	63
39.	Table 35 : Correlations – Homeless Population	66
40.	Table 36 : Correlations – Housed Population	67
41.	Table 37 : Multiple Regression Analyses for External Behavioral Problems	68
42.	Table 38 : Multiple Regression Analyses for Internal Behavioral Problems	69
43.	Table 39 : Multiple Regression Analyses for Total Behavioral Problems	69
44.	Table 40 : Multiple Regression Analyses for – Anxiety Self-concept	70
45.	Table 41 : Multiple Regression Analyses for – Behavior Self-concept	70
46.	Table 42 : Multiple Regression Analyses for – Happiness Self-concept	71
47.	Table 43 : Multiple Regression Analyses for – Intelligence and School Status Self-concept	71
48.	Table 44 : Multiple Regression Analyses for – Physical Self-concept	72
49.	Table 45 : Multiple Regression Analyses for – Popularity Self-concept	72
50.	Table 46 : Multiple Regression Analyses for – Global Self-concept	73

List of Abbreviations

AFDC - Aid to Families with Dependent Children

CBCL - Child Behavior Checklist

DHS - Department of Human Services

DSS - Department of Social Services

FES - Family Environment Scale

FSS - Family Support Scale

GED - General Equivalent Diploma

PDI - Parenting Dimensions Inventory

Piers-Harris-CSCS - Piers-Harris-Children's Self-concept Scale

SES - Socioeconomic Status

SEQ - Social Embeddedness Scale

TANF - Temporary Assistance to Needy Families

HOMELESSNESS AND ITS CONSEQUENCES

Chapter 1

Homelessness – A Historical Perspective

While a place to call home is assured for most individuals, many children are born into the world only to spend their early years without such an affiliation. Also many suffer the loss of their stable base — their homes, due to negative life experiences over which they have no control. These homeless children are born and raised in fragmented family structures that rob them of a fair chance at life from the very start.

Demographic descriptions of homeless families do not tell the whole story about homeless families, but they do begin to indicate the reasons why this phenomenon will not easily or quickly disappear. Prior to the 1980s, the last great surge of homelessness occurred during the Great Depression in the 1930s. As it is today, there were no definite counts of the numbers of Depression-era homeless; estimates ranged from 200,000 to 1.5 million homeless persons in the worst years of Depression (Rossi, 1990). The Depression transient homeless consisted mainly of young men (and a small portion of women) who moved from place to place seeking employment. The majority of the Depression-era homeless left their parental homes because they no longer wanted to be burdens to their already impoverished households and because there were no employment opportunities in their depressed hometowns. Some were urged to leave their parents who were struggling to feed and house their younger siblings. This group of homeless individuals disappeared within months due to a sharp increase in employment opportunities after the war. But the phenomenon of homelessness did not disappear entirely.

The 1950s and 1960s research on homelessness contain no mention of homeless families mainly because many of the social researchers still defined the homeless as familyless. Rossi (1990) describes the homeless in terms of the "old" and the "new" homeless. The "old" homeless of the 1950s were mainly old men living in cheap motels, frequenting inexpensive restaurants and bars on skid rows. The "new" homeless are much younger, more likely to be minority group members, suffering from greater poverty, who had access to mainly poorer sleeping quarters. Bogue (1963) counted 12,000 homeless persons in Chicago in 1958, almost all of them men. Bahr and Caplow (1974) estimated that there were 8,000 homeless men living in New York's Bowery and in 1960, Blumberg, Shipley and Shandler (1973) found that about 2,000 homeless persons were living in the skid row of Philadelphia. The problem of homelessness persisted, still consisting mainly of single male adults.

While the "old" homeless slept in cheap hotels, the "new" homeless were seen sleeping in doorways, in cardboard boxes, in abandoned cars, in railroad or bus stations, or in other public places. In addition, the appearance of homeless women increased significantly. Soon entire families began to show up among the homeless. Women and their children began to seek aid for shelter from public welfare departments (Rossi, 1990). It was unlikely that families appearing on the streets of skid row would be viewed as homeless (Rossi, 1994). The change in the definition of homelessness during the 1970s brought about a dramatic shift in demographic composition of the homeless population as the appearance of homeless families began to emerge.

Throughout the 1980s and into the 1990s the number of homeless families in the United States has continued to grow. Homeless families are comprised primarily of young single parents and their minor children (Kondratas, 1991). Ninety percent of homeless families with children are female-headed households with a mean of two children per family (Kondratas, 1991). Homeless women are more likely to be members of a minority group, and more often dependent on welfare. Homeless women are much younger than homeless men (Dail, 1993). Approximately 50% of the female heading homeless families are between the ages of 17 and 25 years old; 48% white, 45% black and 7% other. Only 10% report being married; the remaining 90% were never married, separated, divorced or widowed (Dail, 1993). Families with children represent the fastest growing segment of the homeless, accounting for approximately 43% of the homeless population (U.S. Conference of Mayors, 1993).

Chapter II

Homelessness Today

A study of the profile of homelessness in New York City, conducted by Homes for the Homeless (1992), found the following: (1) almost 100% of 400 homeless families were headed by single women the majority of whom were under age 25; (2) families had an average of two children; (3) 20% of the families had at least one child in foster care; (4) almost 45% of the families had never been primary tenants, and an additional 25% had been evicted from their last apartment primarily as a result of obvious financial problems; and (4) the majority of families lacked strong support systems or the adjustment living skills necessary to face the challenges of urban poverty. Approximately one-third of the families headed by women are living below the federal poverty level and they are generally poorer than families of aged or disabled persons (Bassuk, 1993). Many homeless women have inadequate education, poor learning power, and limited job opportunities.

To expand on the profile of the homeless beyond mere demographics, Bassuk and Rosenberg (1988) found that maternal drug and alcohol abuse, psychological problems and a history of child abuse as children and battering as adults were much greater among the homeless than was found among mothers living in public or private subsidized housing. Winkelby (1990) reported that homeless mothers show a greater likelihood of having no health insurance coverage, having no preventive health care, and being smokers than is found among the domiciled poor. A large number have been physically and sexually abused as children as well as in adulthood, and some have psychiatric and substance abuse problems (Bassuk, 1993).

Families that become homeless have much lower social support than do other families that never became homeless (Dornbusch, 1994; Letiecq et al., 1996). Prior to becoming homeless, families usually reside in much more crowded housing when sharing with other individuals such as relatives, friends, and sometimes strangers. The crowding that is typical when the homeless stay with relatives often results in family discord: 27% of homeless parents reported that family discord was the reason for their homelessness (Dornbusch, 1994). These findings indicate that homeless parents are at significant risk of having immediate personal issues that require effective intervention or their ability to provide quality parenting will be minimized. This, in turn, places the children at risk for negative physical, cognitive, and social outcomes.

A study conducted by McCormic and Holden (1992) provided information about homeless parents and their children to preschool personnel from the perspective of parents, shelter directors, and their colleagues (other preschool personnel). To assist preschool personnel and other professionals in their work with homeless children, homeless parents provided candid responses about what preschool personnel need to know about homeless preschool children. Parents of preschoolers revealed that: (1) children are embarrassed about being homeless; (2) parents are dealing with many problems in addition to homelessness and their children's care; (3) even parents who may seem distracted really care about their children (just as much as parents in permanent housing); (4) it is very stressful, difficult, and time consuming to have to organize transportation daily; and (5) being homeless does not necessarily mean that the family is dysfunctional.

Shelter directors wanted early childhood personnel to know that: (1) homeless children are especially in need of help with social skills; (2) the reason many parents may not seem to be nurturing is that they do not know how to nurture because they were not nurtured themselves as children (McCormic and Holden, 1992).

Preschool personnel wanted their colleagues to know that: (1) peer friendships among homeless children have to be actively encouraged; (2) stress is unavoidable when one is homeless; some children may seem to be coping but none is impervious to the stress that being homeless places on the family; and (3) even the most basic health and safety concerns may seem overwhelming to already stressed parents (McCormic and Holden, 1992).

PATHWAYS TO HOMELESSNESS

There is no single pathway into homelessness. The myriad of needs that the homeless population present with reflect the variety of experiences that propel them into homelessness. McChesney's (1986a, 1986b) work at the University of Southern California examined the reasons for the current crisis among homeless families. She documented a relationship between increased numbers of low-income families and the decrease in low-cost housing. Her study found that families became homeless because of precipitating events that centered around two themes; economics and relationship crisis. Therefore, homeless children are often exposed to chronic poverty and family discord. This affirms the findings of Dornbusch (1994) that a significant proportion of homeless parents reported that family discord was the reason for their homelessness. Homeless children are often exposed to family discord and always exposed to extreme poverty. Poverty robs the children of adequate education, housing, and health care which are some key elements of the development of a healthy psychological well-being. Family discord creates an unstable and potentially unsafe environment for the children causing a lack of security, another main ingredient for a healthy psychological well-being.

Weitzman, Knickman, and Shinn (1990) found that among 482 homeless adults in New York City, there were three distinct pathways into homelessness: (1) those whose longest residence in the year prior to requesting shelter was a primary tenant (43%); (2) those who lived with others the year before but had once been primary tenants for a year or more (13%); and (3) those who had never had a stable place of their own (44%). The high percentage of those who have resided with others reflect that homeless families have a strong history of residential instability, limited autonomy, and little to no self-sufficiency. This exposes the children to a lack of consistency, poor parental role models as providers, and they are likely to experience a lack of a sense of belonging.

The Weitzman et al. (1990) study was limited to examining housing related pathways, but if earlier pathways that lead to the housing related pathways were identified the issues might have been quite different from solely a housing crisis. To identify these pathways the question would be, "What makes these families more vulnerable than others to a housing crisis?" "What are the events that culminated into their residence in a shelter or motel for the homeless?" It is believed that these different pathways would show that homelessness is only a part of a more complex problem, exposing homeless parents and children to issues other than economically based ones.

A testimony before the United States House of Representatives (1987) identified earlier pathways into homelessness. According to this testimony, teen parents made up a significant number of homeless families seeking shelter (50% in Boston during 1985 and 20% in San Antonio, Texas). Many of these parents were "graduates" of the child welfare system. Homeless children are at risk for similar outcomes. One study reported that of the participating homeless families, 20% had at least one child in foster care (Homes for the Homeless, 1992), and this testimony before the United States House of Representatives (1987) reported that teen parents made up a significant number of homeless families. The question is; "Are the primary problems of these teenagers that of economics or are there other challenges that they face?" It is safe to assume that as participants of the Child Welfare system that there may be issues, such as neglect or abuse, that they are dealing with that may play a role in their resulting homelessness. The strongly proposed position is, homelessness is not solely an economic issue.

Bassuk and Rosenberg (1988) provided further evidence that the issue of homelessness goes beyond economic deprivation. They found in a comparative study with homeless and housed low-income mothers in Boston, Massachusetts that as children, the homeless mothers experienced broken homes (departing fathers) more than housed mothers (29% versus 48%). The homeless more frequently experienced child abuse and 48% of the homeless mothers willing to respond versus 12% of the housed mothers were under investigation for child abuse and neglect. Three-fourths of the homeless mothers indicated that the children's fathers had no relationship at any time with them or that the relationship had ended, compared to 44% of the housed mothers. The homeless mothers reported less meaningful relationships with men than the housed mothers. Fourteen percent of the homeless reported no relationship and 30% described two or more; in contrast 5% of the housed mothers had none and 64% had two or more. Of the men with whom the homeless had relationships, two-thirds had poor work histories, substance abuse problems, battering tendencies, or other problems, in contrast to one-third of the most recent boyfriends of the housed mothers. Forty-two percent of the homeless respondents reported a relationship in which they had been battered, compared to 20% of the housed mothers. Thirty-three percent of the homeless compared to 12% of the housed mothers had substance abuse or psychiatric problems, and 14% of the homeless versus 9% of the housed mothers had been in jail. A history of being abused as a child or adult and a history of substance abuse or psychiatric difficulties were positively correlated with homelessness. This clear distinction between the two groups (housed and homeless) supports the position that the pathways to homelessness are more complex than lack of funds. The findings of Bassuk and Rosenberg (1988) reflect that, in comparison to housed families, poorer interpersonal relationships, disadvantaged backgrounds, poorer parenting quality, higher rates of substance abuse, and higher rates of domestic violence exist among the homeless.

Wagner and Pervine (1994) examined risk factors among homeless women and women at risk of homelessness in a middle sized city in the southeast (population of 225,000). Of the women, 90% were Caucasian, 10% African American, mirroring the racial mix of the city. They found that compared to 48 at-risk housed women, 50 homeless women reported a history of more symptoms of mental illness, more instability of employment and housing, more physical and sexual abuse, more drug and alcohol problems, and fewer skills for interacting with others. When compared to women who were homeless for less than six months, those who were homeless for longer than six months were less educated, younger when they first became pregnant, and more likely to abuse alcohol, to have been assaulted, and to have attempted suicide. Studies have also shown that approximately 30% of homeless women have substance abuse problems (Fisher, 1991; Fisher and Breakey, 1987).

Homeless parents have also been found to be more isolated, and have less social support than housed parents (Dornbusch, 1994). The reason for the isolation may stem from the mothers' own childhood. Studies of homeless mothers have documented a relatively high frequency of early and current disruptive experiences, including divorce, desertion, illness, parental death or victimization (Bassuk, 1991). Lack of social support makes raising a family, for the already emotionally drained, even more difficult. Recurring negative experiences, namely desertion, abuse, illness, and conflict experienced by the parents will directly affect the quality of the social experiences the parents have with their children. It is very likely that if the parents have negative experiences their social interactions with their children will also be negative.

One pathway into homelessness that is found to be quite common is domestic violence. Women are found to be more likely than men to be homeless because of family stress, particularly domestic violence (Hagen and Ivanoff, 1988) One-third of homeless women interviewed in Portland, Oregon, were homeless due to them leaving an abusive relationship (Anderson, Boe, and Smith, 1988). Twenty-two percent of homeless women in Albany, New York listed domestic violence as a key factor leading to their homelessness (Hagen and Ivanoff, 1988).

Scientific research also shows that early experiences, for example family history and childhood experiences appear to be directly related to homelessness. More homeless women than men have been raised in institutional care and have been sexually abused as a child (Anderson et. al., 1988; Bassuk, Rubin and Lauriat, 1986; Crystal, 1984; D'Ercole and Strueming, 1987). Bassuk and Rosenberg (1988) also reported that the homeless more frequently experience child abuse than the housed.

As reflected by these findings, there is no one route to homelessness, as there is no one effect of its consequences. No one story can describe all the broad ranges of experiences and life conditions that lead to homelessness, but some distinct pathways that typify the trajectory of most families can be identified.

CHAPTER III

The Multidimensional Effects of Homelessness

IMPACT OF HOMELESSNESS ON PARENTS

Poverty, and more pronounced homelessness, imposes ongoing stress on families. It is a stressful experience when parents cannot provide their children's basic needs, for example, adequate health care, adequate education, safe neighborhoods, and socially and culturally enriching activities. Becoming homeless, for whatever reason, is an immediate stressor, and becoming rehoused is a herculean task that can elicit ongoing and increased stress. As postulated by Maslow (1954) the basic needs must be adequately met first before those at the higher levels can be met. Since the basic needs of the homeless for food, shelter, and safety are not adequately met, homeless parents may be more concerned with meeting their own and their children's basic needs and less concerned with those at the higher levels, such as the emotional needs of their children.

McLoyd (1990) provided support for the person-process-context model espoused by Bronfenbrenner (1986). This model describes the impact of economic hardship on family processes as a function of personal characteristics of individual family members, including the child (See Figure 3).

McLoyd (1990) proposed that the principal assumptions of the model are that:

"(a) poverty and economic loss diminish the capacity for supportive, consistent, and involved parenting; (b) a major mediator of the link between economic hardship and parenting behavior is psychological distress deriving from an excess of negative life events, undesirable chronic conditions, and the absence and disruption of marital bonds; (c) economic loss and poverty indirectly affect children through their impact on the parents' behavior toward the child; and (d) father-child relations under conditions of economic hardship depend on the quality of relations between the mother and father." (McLoyd, 1990, p. 312).

Figure 3. Analytic Model of how Poverty and Economic Loss Affect Children (McLoyd, 1990).

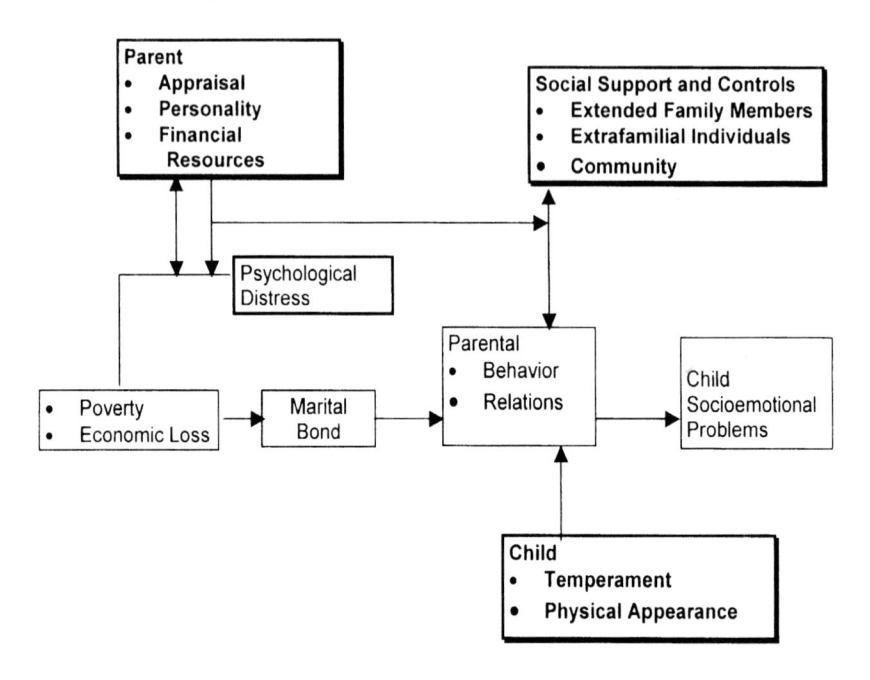

```
┌─────────────────────┐
│ Parent              │
│ • Appraisal         │          ┌──────────────────────────┐
│ • Personality       │          │ Social Support and Controls │
│ • Financial         │          │ • Extended Family Members │
│   Resources         │          │ • Extrafamilial Individuals│
└─────────────────────┘          │ • Community              │
                                 └──────────────────────────┘
        ┌──────────────┐
        │ Psychological│
        │ Distress     │
        └──────────────┘
                        ┌──────────────┐
                        │ Parental     │
                        │ • Behavior   │         ┌──────────────┐
┌────────────┐ ┌──────┐ │ • Relations  │         │ Child        │
│ • Poverty  │→│Marital│→│              │───────→│ Socioemotional│
│ • Economic │ │Bond  │ │              │         │ Problems     │
│   Loss     │ └──────┘ └──────────────┘         └──────────────┘
└────────────┘
                        ┌──────────────┐
                        │ Child        │
                        │ • Temperament│
                        │ • Physical Appearance │
                        └──────────────┘
```

If poverty and economic loss are main influences on parenting behavior, then homeless parents are at high risk of negative parenting behavior. Also, if negative life events precipitate psychological distress, then due to the ongoing negative experiences of the homeless, homeless parents are predisposed to negative parenting behaviors.

Other research has been consistent with the person-process-context model. Bronfenbrenner (1986) reported that stressful experiences increase psychological distress in mothers and produce changes in family and child-management practices. Distressed mothers were found to use increased adverse, coercive discipline that in turn contributed to antisocial behavior in the children (Patterson, DeBarsyshe, and Ramsey, 1989; Patterson, 1988).

Economic decline, poverty, and lower-class status, all of which typify the homeless, are marked by relatively punitive and coercive patterns of parenting behavior. In a number of theoretical frameworks, the underlying cause is said to be psychological distress in parents (Gecas, 1979).

A direct source of psychological distress for all involved is homelessness. Shelter living can be a disadvantage and a source of stress to the mothers. The majority of the staff from 25 shelters reported that the mothers were often depressed when in the shelters and they often had feelings of guilt, fear, and anger (Huttman and Redmond, 1992). These feelings of guilt, depression, fear, and anxiety are likely to generate negative self-perceptions among the mothers and negative parent-child relationships.

The perception of or the way in which the homeless interpret their experiences further explicates why many experience guilt, depression, fear and anxiety. Seven themes of homelessness emerged from the findings of a study of how 15 mothers living in three homeless shelters interpreted their experiences (Bauman, 1993). Unstructured interviews and conversations were the means of information gathering. The seven themes of homelessness are as follows: boundaries, connections, fatigue/despair, self-respect, lack of self-determination, privacy, and mobility.

The homeless mothers reported that they lacked self-determination, self-respect, and privacy, that they felt fatigue/despair, and that there were minimal boundaries and privacy in the shelters. The mothers also reported that it was difficult for them to share their meaning systems with their children because they did not have their own place, and other social connections were strained when they attempted socially meaningful interactions with their children (Bauman, 1993).

The children also experience the effects of homelessness and its negative concomitants. A comparison of homeless and domiciled adolescents (ages 13 to 18 years) revealed that the homeless adolescents reported the highest incidence of marital discord, and lowest levels of parental care and acceptance (Dadds, Braddock, Cuers, and Elliott, 1993). Homeless adolescents (mean age 15.54 years) were also found to be significantly more deprived emotionally, socially, and culturally than their comparison group — domiciled adolescents (Kinzlel, 1993; Schweitzer, Hier, and Terry, 1994).

Substantial findings report that stressful life events experienced by parents are related to parents' depressed moods that operate to disrupt skillful parenting practices. The disrupted parenting practices place children at risk for developing depressive symptoms (Ge, Conger, Lorenz, and Simmons, 1994).

The actual experiences of homelessness may not be the sole contributing factors to impaired parental functioning. Homeless families struggle with a double crisis, the loss of a home as well as impediments to the parents' ability to function as a consistent and supportive caregiver. Other traumatizing and belittling experiences could be the inability to establish a stable home for the family and the parents' inability to change that situation and become a consistent provider. The experience of homelessness is likely to disrupt the parents' capacity to provide for the children's needs and to protect and support them (Hausman and Hammen, 1993).

Some specific psychological stressors, namely; poverty, unemployment, low education levels, and substance abuse have been found to place families at risk of child abuse (Newberger, Hampton, Marx, and White, 1986; Oates, 1986). Poverty has been recognized as a correlate of child abuse, however the relationship between the two is not understood. But the person-process-context model (Bronfenbrenner, 1986) could serve as a possible explanation. Pelton (1981) has suggested that the problems associated with poverty such as unemployment, inadequate housing, and low education levels, provide a context for abuse. According to Pelton (1981), living in such conditions may generate stressful experiences that may lead to child abuse.

Stress is closely associated with both depression and anxiety (Steinberg, Catalano, and Dooley, 1981). As parents experience depressed moods they may become decreasingly effective in handling discipline situations. For example, in situations where the parents have the potential for child abuse, oppositional behaviors or difficult temperament, might be stressful enough to precipitate an abusive incident.

It is impossible to separate homelessness from poverty, psychological stress, and negative life experiences. All these factors have been found to be associated with negative parental behaviors, and in some cases child abuse. Koblinsky, Morgan and Anderson (1997) compared the parenting practices of homeless and housed mothers of preschoolers, and found that homeless mothers exhibited significantly poorer parenting behavior on several measures. Specifically, the researchers found that homeless mothers, in comparison to housed low-income mothers, provided less learning and academic stimulation, less variety in social and cultural experiences, less warmth and affection, and less positive physical environment for their children.

Parenting Stress and Quality

Parenting stress, which is defined as the relative magnitude of stress in the parent-child system (Abidin, 1983) is a main factor that hinders healthy parent-child relationships and minimizes emotional support from the parents. Research on parenting suggests that one major factor that contribute to the mother's level of stress is stressful life events. Stressful life events include demographic conditions, such as limited resources, as well as adverse life changes. In a study by Conger, McCarthy, Yans, Lahey, and Kropp (1984), 53% of the variance in parenting stress could be accounted for by stressful demographic conditions such as family income and number of children. Other research has shown limited income resources and uncertainty about financial situations to be the primary sources of stress in a group of low-income mothers (Belle, 1982).

It is well established that stress is a mediator in the parenting process, but more specifically, contextual sources of stress are major mediating factors in the parenting process and can directly or indirectly influence children's development (Belsky, 1984). The research that supports this position has typically involved the assessment of the adverse impact of difficult life circumstances such as poverty and low socioeconomic status (Belle, 1981; Werner and Smith, 1982), parental psychopathology (Garmezy, Masten, and Telleger, 1984; Sameroff and Seifer, 1983), child psychopathology (Mash and Johnston, 1983), major childhood illness or handicap (Beckman, 1983), and major negative life changes (Crnic, Greenberg, Regozin, Robinson, and Basham, 1983). In general, greater stress is significantly associated with less optimal parent and family functioning, less optimal parent-child interactions, and lower child developmental competence (McLoyd, 1990; Raschke and Raschke, 1979; Straus, 1980).

It has been made clear that major life stressors are negatively related to various aspects of the parent, child, and family system; however, research also suggests that major life stresses are low frequency occurrences for most families (Crnic and Greenberg, 1987). Lazarus and his colleagues (Kanner, Coyne, Schaefer, and Lazarus, 1981; Lazarus, 1984; Lazarus, Cohen, Folkman, Kanner, and Schaefer, 1980) have also questioned the utility of the major life event approach, and proposed that the cumulative impact of relatively minor daily stress ("daily hassles") may have major impact.

Within any family, the ongoing routine challenges of childrearing and caregiving is inevitable. Isolated cases of being nagged or whined at, settling arguments between siblings and cleaning up messes, as well as a myriad of other possible everyday events will occur. But their cumulative impact over a day, several days, or longer may constitute a meaningful stressor for a parent. Parents' evaluation of these events and their significance may have important implications for parental, family, and child functioning.

Hassles are thought of as the irritating, frustrating, annoying, and distressing demands that to some degree characterize everyday transactions within the environment (Crnic and Greenberg, 1987). Some hassles may be situationally determined and frequent (as it is with having to deal with the many rules of family shelter on a daily basis), while others may be repetitive because the individual remains in the context with consistent predictable demands. Any single event may or may not constitute a hassle, but the cumulative impact of these events may adversely affect parent-child relationships.

Patterson (1983) has shown that minor daily hassles experienced by mothers predicted irritable responses to their children during home observations, which, in turn, increased the likelihood of aggressive responding by their children. Dumas (1986) has also found that mothers interacted significantly more aversively with their children on days when they had experienced aversive interactions with adults than on days in which they had not.

Scientific research has shown that there are interrelationships among parenting stress, parental psychological symptomatology, and parenting behavior. Rodgers (1993) found that among a random sample of 85 mothers and children in Head Start and kindergarten: (1) parenting stress both directly and indirectly affected parenting behavior, (2) parenting stress directly affected parental symptomatology, and (3) parental psychological symptomatology directly affected parenting behavior.

In addition to the parent behavior, parental stress has direct effects on the parents' self-esteem. Lower role satisfaction and lower maternal self-esteem has been found to be directly related to parental stress (Koeske and Koeske, 1990). If a mother is dissatisfied with her parental role and has low self-esteem there is a strong likelihood that these negative feelings will be reflected in her relationship with her child(ren), which is likely to negatively affect the child(ren)'s psychological well-being.

Based on research findings, homelessness is clearly a negative life event that is characterized by chronic stress. Children who are subject to parents who are challenged by these stressors are at risk of negative social experiences with their parents, negative parenting practices, and hence, compromised psychological well-being.

Social Support

A leading buffer for families in stress, particularly in the area of parenting, is social support (Dornbusch, 1994; Hashima and Amato, 1994). Dornbusch (1994) and Hashima and Amato (1994) found that social support was negatively associated with parents' reports of punitive behavior toward children, but mainly when income is low. It has been found that mothers' social support moderates the effects of daily hassles of parenting (Crnic and Greenberg, 1987). Further analyses indicated that higher maternal social support positively moderated the influence of parenting hassles on indices of negative maternal behavior. Mothers who are satisfied with their social support praise their children more and are less controlling than dissatisfied mothers (Jennings, Stagg, and Connors, 1991). In addition, other studies have shown that socially isolated families have higher rates of child abuse than do other families (Corse, Schmid, and Trickett, 1990; Gelles and Straus, 1979; Hunter and Kilstrom, 1979; Kotch and Thomas, 1986; Salzinger, Kaplan, and Artemyeff, 1983; Straus, 1980; Wolock and Harowitz, 1979).

Rodgers (1993) examined the relationship of social support to parenting stress, parenting behavior, and parental psychological symptomatology among mothers of children in Head Start and kindergarten and found that social support buffered the relationship between parenting stress and parenting behavior, and between parental psychological symptomatology and parenting behavior.

Social support is said to positively affect parenting behavior/functioning. Research has reported this on specific and general domains. A specific aspect of parenting behavior (quality of stimulation in the home) was examined in relation to social support. It was found that higher social support is positively related to this aspect of parenting behavior (Parks, Lenz, and Jenkins, 1992). In the general domain, social support, particularly informal social support, is reported by Roggman, Moe, Hart, and Forthun (1994) to positively affect parental functioning for parents of Head Start children; no specific domain was examined.

As reflected in the literature social support plays a key role in the lives of parents — it provides a buffer for parental stress and therefore may facilitate the psychological well-being of children. However, the availability of social support to the homeless is often nonexistent or at a minimum (Solarz and Bogat, 1990).

IMPACT OF HOMELESSNESS ON CHILDREN

Physical Implications

Studies have consistently found that homeless children experience elevated levels of acute and chronic health problems (Rafferty and Shinn, 1991). Health risks begin before birth. A comparison was made between the reproductive experiences of 401 homeless females in welfare hotels in New York City with that of 13,249 females in public housing and with all live births in New York City during the same time period (Homes for the Homeless, 1992). It was found that significantly more of the homeless females (16%, versus 11% of females in public housing and 7% of all females) had low birth-weight babies. Infant mortality was also high: 25 deaths per 1,000 live births among the homeless females compared with 17 per 1,000 for housed poor women, and 12 per 1,000 for women city wide. Of the 401 homeless females 60% received even minimal prenatal care, compared to 85% of the public housing residents, and 91% of all other New York City women.

The Homeless Health Care Project in California showed that homeless children, continually exposed to the elements, "suffer from a high incidence of upper respiratory infections, such as bronchitis or pneumonia, because they sleep in automobiles and other cold, unsuitable places" (Roberts and Henry, 1986). Miller and Linn (1988) surveyed the health status of 158 homeless children living in the state of Washington and found the incidence of health problems to be four times higher than estimates of the general U.S. pediatric population. Alperstein, Rappalation, and Flanigan (1988) reviewed the medical records of homeless children under age five, they found that delayed immunizations, elevated blood levels, hospital admissions, and incidence of neglect and abuse were all greater than in a comparison sample of low socioeconomic status (SES) children attending the same New York clinic.

Wright (1987, 1990, 1991) examined the medical records of 1,028 homeless children under 15 years of age who were treated in the Robert Wood Johnson Health Care for the homeless program in 16 cities. In his comparison of the occurrence of various diseases and disorders among homeless children with rates reported in the National Ambulatory Medical

Care Survey for U.S. ambulatory patients ages 15 and under, he found that all disorders studied were more common among homeless children. The occurrence of these disorders was often double the rate observed in the general pediatric caseload. The common disorders among homeless children were upper respiratory infections (42% vs. 22% in the national sample), minor skin ailments (20% vs. 5% in the national sample), ear disorders (18% vs. 12% in the national sample), chronic physical disorders (15% vs. 9% in the national sample), and gastrointestinal disorders (15% vs. 4% in the national sample). Infestational ailments although less common than other disorders among homeless children (7%), occurred more than 53 times the rate of those in the national sample.

Alperstein and Arnstein (1988) and Alperstein, et al. (1988) made several comparisons between the health of homeless children in New York City and the health of poor housed children receiving health care there. They found that 27% of 265 homeless children less than 5 years of age residing in "welfare" hotels were late in getting necessary immunizations, compared with 8% of 100 poor children attending the same outpatient clinic. Twice as many homeless children (4%) as members of the population of 1,072 children (2%) whose blood was tested that year by the clinic (2%), had elevated lead levels in the blood. Rates of hospital admission among a larger sample of 2,500 homeless children under the age of 18 were 11.6 per thousand vs. 4.5 per thousand for children of the same age living in the same area; more than a two-to-one ratio.

Bernstein et al. (1988) compared the clinic charts of 90 homeless children ages six months through 12 years with those of a matched cohort of housed children with family incomes below the federal poverty level. Approximately 48% of the homeless children under age two years were delayed in their immunizations, compared with 16% of the housed children. Fifty percent of the homeless children, compared with 25% of the housed group, had iron deficiencies.

Other studies, such as those of Wright (1990, 1991) and Wood, Valdez, Hayashi, and Shen (1990a) report that homeless children's health problems include immunization delays, asthma, ear infections, overall poor health, diarrhea, and anemia.

Psychological and Developmental Implications

While homelessness has negative psychological effects on the parents and the parent-child relationship, it also has a similar and direct impact on the children. The impact of homelessness on children is illustrated in case reports described in a study conducted by Bassuk (1986) at Harvard Medical School. Martha and her family were among the families interviewed. Martha's five-month-old daughter, Sarah is frail, listless and underweight. She cannot hold down her food, cannot grasp a rattle, and rarely smiles or vocalizes. Martha's fifteen-month-old son has moved seven times since he was born and is painfully shy. Since arrival at the shelter he has stopped exercising his limited vocabulary, refused eating, and has had trouble sleeping. Five-month-old Sarah and 15-month-old Matthew are members of a group of highly victimized homeless children.

The consequences of homelessness on children are dire. Homelessness robs children during their critical, formative years of the basic resources needed for normal development. A home gives a sense of security, belongingness, organization, and predictability — these are benefits that homeless children do not experience. Instead, they undergo events that contribute to medical, emotional, and behavioral problems that may be of lasting duration.

The most comprehensive look at children as primary victims of homelessness was conducted by Bassuk (1984). Her work with children living in family shelters in Massachusetts showed that nearly half of those studied evidenced one major developmental delay, while one-third had evidence of two major developmental delays. Most of the children also showed evidence of high levels of anxiety, severe depression, and learning difficulties, and half appeared to require psychiatric evaluation. Homeless children also presented with more sleep problems, shyness, withdrawal, and aggression, compared to same age peers who are not homeless and diagnosed with emotional disturbance (Bassuk and Rubin, 1987). Bassuk and Rosenberg (1990) also found that almost half of the pre-school children tested manifested serious emotional and developmental delays. When compared with poor, housed children, homeless children were slower in language development, motor skills, fine motor coordination and personal and social ability.

Grant (1990) conducted a study that described the demographics of 72 homeless families and 87 homeless preschoolers in a day care at a large welfare hotel in New York. He found that severe separation problems, characterized by panic states, hysterical crying, vomiting, and severe anxiety interfering with the ability to participate in routine activities; poor quality (superficial) relationships, sleep disturbances, and short attention span were present among approximately three-quarters of the children. Grant (1990) also found signs of emotional disturbance including severe tantrums, dangerously aggressive and destructive behavior, extreme withdrawal, violent mood swings, and oppositional and manipulative behaviors serious enough to interfere with peer relationships and readiness to learn. Significant delays were found in gross motor development (particularly problems in movement through space and spatial relations), speech and language development (particularly restrictions in expressive language and vocabulary development), and cognitive development (particularly with tasks requiring sequencing and organization).

The Senate Subcommittee on Children, Families, Drugs, and Alcoholism has had testimony from several witnesses working with homeless children

(Landers, 1989). For example, the health commissioner of Fulton County, Georgia, reported that homeless children do not attend school regularly, lack immunizations, have chronic health problems, and suffer from anxiety and disturbed relationships.

Bassuk and Rosenberg (1990) compared homeless and domiciled children and found that significantly more homeless than domiciled children under age five manifested one or more developmental delays, (54% versus 16%); however, the proportion of preschool children attending daycare was similar in both groups (36% and 32%). Homeless and comparison groups of preschool children did not differ significantly on behavior problems according to the Simmons Behavior Checklist (SBC). Differences between school-aged homeless and comparison group children on the Child Behavior Checklist (CBC-L), the Children's Manifest Anxiety Scale (CMAS), and the Children's Depression Inventory (CDI) were not significant, although the homeless children generally had higher scores.

In a study conducted by Bassuk and Rosenberg (1988) of homeless children in the Boston area, it was found that on the Children's Depression Inventory (CDI), the mean total score of the homeless children was 10.3 compared to 8.3 for the housed children. A cut off point of 9.0 indicates a need for psychiatric evaluation. On the Children's Manifest Anxiety Scale, 31% of the homeless children tested compared to 9% of the housed children had a T-score of 60 or higher, indicating the need for psychiatric referral and evaluation.

Bassuk et al. (1986) examined 151 homeless children ranging in age from 6 weeks to 18 years and 81 homeless children age five years and under in a study. Forty-seven percent of the five year olds or younger had at least one developmental lag and 33% had two or more developmental lags. On the Simmons Behavior Checklist, 55 children ages three to five years scored higher than the overall mean of 5.6 on the following factors: shyness (9.6), dependent behavior (7.4), aggression (7.4), attention span (7.3), withdrawal (6.1), and demanding behavior (5.7). They scored less than the mean on sleep problems (4.5), coordination (4.1), fear of new things (3.8), and speech difficulties (3.5). The findings on the Children's Depression Inventory and the Children's Manifest Anxiety Scale reflect that, of the 52 children older than five years who were tested, approximately half required further psychiatric evaluation. Based on the Achenbach parent checklist, of the 29 six to eleven year olds, two-thirds of the boys and almost one-half of the girls required further psychiatric evaluation; of the 13 children, ages 12 through 16, more than one-third required psychiatric referral.

Zeisemer et al. (1994) examined the differences in academic performance, adaptive functioning, and problem behaviors of 145 elementary school-age children who had experienced homelessness and a matched group of 142 mobile children with low socioeconomic status (SES). No significant differences were found between homeless and low SES-mobile children on academic performance, adaptive functioning, and problem behaviors. Homeless and low SES-mobile children did not differ from each other on behavior and socioemotional problems. However, teachers perceived them as having substantially more problems in these areas than the norm group of students from families in the lowest SES categories.

Molnar (1988) documented teachers' accounts of behaviors of much concern of preschoolers between the ages of two and a half to five years in New York City. The behaviors most frequently noted include short attention span, withdrawal, aggression, speech delays, sleep disorders, "regressive" toddlerlike behaviors, inappropriate social interaction with adults, immature peer interaction, contrasted with strong sibling relationships, and immature motor behavior.

Rescorla, Parker, and Stolley (1991) conducted a comparative study with homeless and domiciled disadvantaged children. They found that school-aged children in both groups did not differ significantly on most measures of cognition and adjustment behaviors. However, preschool homeless children exhibited slower development and more emotional and behavioral problems than their domiciled peers, and significantly fewer were enrolled in early childhood programs.

Educational Implications

Estimates of the number of school-aged homeless children in this country range from 220,000 to as many as 750,000 (U.S. Department of Education, 1989; and National Coalition for the Homeless, 1987, respectively). Estimates of their school attendance rates range from as low as 43% (National Coalition for the Homeless, 1987) to 57% (Maza and Hall, 1988) to as high as 70% (U.S. Department of Education, 1989). Rafferty and Rollins (1989) conducted a study in New York City and reported attendance rates by grade level clusters for 6,433 homeless children and compared them to the attendance rates of all New York City public school attendance. As the grade level increased, attendance rates declined for all students. The homeless children had poorer attendance at all levels, and their attendance rates declined at a faster rate than for students in the system as a whole. Attendance rates for homeless versus all students, respectively, in the New York City system were as follows: 73.6% vs. 88.7% at the elementary level, 63.6% vs. 85.5% at the junior high level, and 50.9% vs. 83.9% at the high school level.

Bassuk and Rubin (1987) and Molnar, Rath and Klein (1990) found that 25% of their sample of school-age children was in special education classes, and 43% had repeated a grade. Of the sampled school-aged homeless children, Bassuk (1984) found that 45% had repeated at least one grade. Among the school-aged children, rates of being retained in grade, attending special classes, and failing in school were comparable.

Regarding academic performance Zeisemer et al. (1994) found that the reading and mathematics achievement of the homeless and low SES-mobile low-income students did not differ significantly. Approximately one-third of both groups were performing at or above grade level, however, almost two-thirds were below grade level. Approximately 70% of the students in the homeless and low SES-mobile low-income groups were at moderate or greater risk academically or behaviorally. About 10% were at severe risk, and approximately 30% were perceived by teachers to be functioning within the normal range or to have only mild risk factors.

The St. Louis Homeless Children's Project (Whitman, Stretch, and Accardo, 1987) assessed the cognitive language abilities of 107 homeless children, aged five months to 17 years. On the Slosson Intelligence Test Revised, 45% scored at or below the slow learner/borderline range of abilities, a rate three times that of the general population. On the Peabody Vocabulary Test-Revised, 89% of the children tested fell at the 50th percentile or lower.

The Child Welfare League of America and Travelers Aid Society surveyed 33 states; 163 homeless families including 340 children and found that 30% of the children who were attending school had been held back (Maza and Hall, 1988). Bassuk et al. (1986) found that 43% of the homeless in their New England sample were failing or performing below average work; this was almost double the rate of 23% reported by mothers of the 34 low-income housed comparison-group children who were interviewed the following year (Bassuk and Rosenberg, 1988). The Massachusetts data reported by Bassuk et al. (1986) and Bassuk and Rubin (1987) reflected that 25% of the 50 homeless school-aged children in contrast to 10.9% students across the entire American school population were in special education classes.

The academic performance (reading and math scores) of homeless children in New York was examined by Rafferty and Rollins (1989). When compared with the scores of those obtained system wide by domiciled students, less than half (42.3%) of the homeless students, grades three through ten, who took the Degrees of Reading Power test scored at or above grade level, compared to 68.1% of all New York City students who took the test. In math, for students in grades two through eight who took the Metropolitan Achievement Test, 28.1% of homeless students scored at or above grade level, compared to 56.7% of all New York City students who took the test.

The problem associated with educating homeless children were typified in a 1987 Colorado study (Colorado Children's Campaign, 1987) which looked at families and children living in shelters. The study found that 33% of the school aged children reported frequent absences and tardiness.

CONCLUSIONS

A methodology problem with most of the early studies of homeless youngsters was that no comparable data were collected on disadvantaged children from similar population living in a residence (Whitman, Accardo, Boyert, and Kendagor, 1990; Zima, Wells, Freeman, 1994). This is a crucial group, because the inner city children from minority families are known to have a very high base rate of the same medical, educational, developmental, and psychiatric problems that are common among the homeless youngsters (Rescorla et. al., 1991).

Chapter IV

The Formation of Self-concept

The self-concept is acquired, not inherited. One's perception of one's self is based primarily on relationships one has with one's immediate family and other significant figures. Kiester states, "It is the foundation on which personality is built and the primary determinant of behavior." (1973, p.1).

Social psychologists believe that the individual's conception of himself is learned through social interaction. Social psychologists believe the ways in which other people respond to the individual determine how s/he perceives him/herself. If according to Sullivan (1945), Lifshitz (1975), and Killeen (1993), the parents are the primary influence on children's self-concept, then the social interaction that parents have with their children and how they respond to their children are major determinants of the children's self-concept.

The self-concept of young children is of a rudimentary quality. The early formation of young children's self-concept forms a foundation for subsequent development. Young children have but a vague awareness of their self-concept, therefore, they are relatively dependent on adults, usually the parents to provide consistent, understandable reactions to their behaviors in various situations or circumstances. In order for young children to develop their sense of self, they must integrate feelings of security in their dependence on adults with feelings of newly found autonomy and self-control.

The self-concept of homeless children is important for consideration because the self-concept contains representations of our special abilities, achievements, preferences, the unique aspects of our appearance, and the personalized expressions of our temperament (Markus et al., 1982). A diversity of self-relevant information is gained through social experiences and this self-relevant information becomes organized into cognitive structures (Markus et al., 1982). The self-concept of homeless children is a product of social experiences and responses from already emotionally drained parents. The social experiences of homeless children are unique and pervasively negative in that they experience deprivation of things that the average child takes for granted. Their parents, who play the key role in the shaping of their selves' are very likely to be distracted by ongoing stress, they face the stigma of homelessness, and they lack the necessary sense of security and belongingness basic to social identification and development. The cognitive structures that emerge from these social experiences explain the children's feelings about themselves, and the value they place on what they do and their performance in various domains. According to Markus et al. (1982), a combination of these cognitive structures form the self-concept.

Cognitive structures that contribute to the children's self-concept will also result from the way others view them (Cooley, 1902; Mead, 1934; Sullivan, 1945). Cooley coined the term the "looking-glass self" to refer to this aspect of self-concept. Sullivan (1945) takes the position that the most influential in this aspect of self-concept are the children's parents.

PARENTAL INFLUENCES ON CHILDREN'S SELF-CONCEPT

Lifshitz (1975) has proposed that one's sense of identity, or self-concept, develops as a result of a series of successive comparisons and contrasts between self, father, and mother. If it is a single parent family, Lifshitz (1975) proposes that the child should grow away from the departed parent and gravitate to the remaining parent who continues to care for him/her. Parish and Copeland (1979) have reported findings that tend to support Lifshitz' (1975) model. Specifically, Parish and Copeland (1979) found that the self-concepts of college students from intact families did significantly correlate with the self-concept of both their parents, while college students from single parent families headed by their mothers tend to have self-concepts that correlated significantly with the ratings of their mothers and their stepfathers, but not with their fathers.

An investigation of the relationship between children's self-concept and evaluations of parent figure (Nunn and Parish, 1987) was conducted using children in grades five through 10 who came from intact families, divorced families, or families in which one or both parents had died. Significant relations were obtained between children's self-concept ratings and their evaluations of their natural father and mother for both intact and divorced families. The relationship was not significant, however, for families in which a parent had died. Furthermore, children's self-ratings were significantly correlated with their evaluations of stepparents.

Parish and Dostal (1980) had similar findings with younger children — fifth through eighth grades. They reported that children from divorced families expressed self-concepts that were significantly correlated with their evaluations of their mothers not their fathers.

The influence of significant others on the self-concept of children have been supported by scientific findings. Goodman, Adamson, Rimti, and Cole (1994) found that depressed mothers' critical attitudes actively contributed to their children's lower self-esteem. Results also suggest that children's self-esteem and perception of family members are aligned with families' configuration, family processes, and mother-child relationships (Mahaber, 1993).

Considering the challenges that homeless parents face, it is likely that homeless children will have poor self-concepts. Due to the social experiences that precede homelessness and those they incur during homelessness they are likely to have developed negative cognitive structures, which in turn will result in negative self-concepts.

THE INFLUENCE OF HOMELESSNESS ON PARENT-CHILD RELATIONSHIPS

In exploring the reasons for the psychological and developmental consequences of homelessness, Boxill and Beaty (1987) studied mothers and their children living in shelters in Atlanta, Georgia. They learned that homelessness as the context for mother/child relationships forces an "out of order" relationship. That is, this context produces a parent-child relationship that is public, with every aspect of their lives in full public view. The full range of trivial to significant family actions and interactions is open to public intervention. For these families, their private life, for example, eating, bathing, and telephone conversations, become public life with permission from shelter staff. The authors' findings were based on responses from mothers who were unsure of their own parenting ability within this setting and the behaviors of the children in reaction to their current situation, who know only the uncertainty of what tomorrow would bring.

Coopersmith (1967) postulated that there would be a relationship between the parents' self-esteem and that of the children's. He indicated that parents with high self-esteem will be more accepting of others, and would be able to provide the children with a more definite idea of what they expected and desired. Positive correlation between the mothers' self-concepts and that of their children were found by Tocco and Bridges (1973) for kindergartners and first graders and by Baruch (1976) for fifth and tenth grade girls.

Sailor and Crumley (1975) reported that poor women see themselves as being looked down on by everyone because they are on welfare and because most people do not understand poverty. Other mothers reported "The poor are misunderstood because most people associate poverty with being drunk, dirty, and hatching out a kid every five minutes — not worrying about what happens. They do if they haven't been there themselves at some time..." (Sailor & Crumley, 1975, p.7). These are negative social experiences that are very likely to result in negative cognitive structures, hence negative self-concepts.

Homeless parents are inevitably poor, and so, homeless children may be at risk of developing impaired self-concepts due to the emotional state of the parents as a result of their homelessness and poverty. Alternatively, poor self-concepts could be a concomitant of poverty. Previous research has found that impaired self-concept and mothers' strains were inversely related to income, not family type (Nelson, 1993).

Further examination of the parental influence on children's self-concept occurs in the research by Killeen (1993). The findings support a model of the self in which parents (1) influence self-concept by providing children with information on how well they perform in specific domains and which domains are important and (2) influence self-esteem by their affective behavior. Global self-worth was predicted by children's perceptions, parental support and perceived competence in domains that were important to the parents.

Parenting style characterized as caring, empathic, devoid of excessive intrusion and infantilization has been found to correlate with the best family functioning and adolescent well-being (McCullough, Ashbridge and Pegg, 1994; Dickstein and Posner, 1978). This style of parenting was found to be independent of family structure. This finding provides support to the position that the parents have the most influence on the child's self-concept, despite the structure of the family.

Children's perceptions of parental-behavior have also been found to support the position that a relationship exists between the elementary school child's perception of parental acceptance and the child's self-esteem. Studies in this area found (a) a relationship between the child's self-esteem and the quality of parent-child relationships in the male child's view (Dickstein and Posner, 1978); (b) the male child's perception of both parents as loving and not punishing, while, for the female child, the perception of only the mother as loving (Nolan, 1987); (c) the perception of the female child of their mothers as being high on acceptance and nurturance (Graybill, 1978; Hazzard, Christensen and Margolin, 1983); (d) the perception of parents as being accepting in a study of children with and without tourette syndrome (Edell and Motta, 1989); (e) the perception of parents as being accepting and understanding on the part of children with learning disabilities whose parents had participated in a Parent Effectiveness Training program (Gianotti and Doyle, 1982); and (f) satisfaction with communication with their mothers on the part of emotionally disturbed and nondisabled adolescents (Omizo, Amerikaner, and Michael, 1985).

PARENT SELF-CONCEPT, FAMILY FUNCTIONING AND THEIR EFFECTS ON THE PARENTING ROLE AND CHILDREN'S SELF-CONCEPT

A negative self-concept may result in a negative view of the parenting role, which in turn may result in negative social experiences with the children. According to Markus et al. (1982) these negative social experiences with the children can contribute to negative cognitive structures, hence negative self-concept in the children.

Research has shown that internal locus of control, emotional stability, positive communication skills, and positive family interactions are positively related to positive self-esteem (Altmann and Firnesz, 1973; Calsyn, Quicke, and Harris, 1980; Spivak and Shure, 1974). Researchers and clinicians with a family systems theoretical orientation are particularly interested in studying what the perceptions of family interactions are among family members and how these perceptions influence the family members' behaviors. Kaslow and Cooper (1978) placed emphasis on studying variables related to family interaction when working with children in special education. These researchers have also indicated that individuals who perceive that he can communicate easily with family members usually feel better about themselves. Omizo et al. (1985) also found that children, ages 11 to 14, with high Coopersmith Self-esteem Inventory score also had higher levels of positive feelings toward their mothers. Cooper, Holman and Braithwaite (1983) found that children from different family types experienced varying degrees of closeness and support. Furthermore, those children reporting very little family support tended to score low on self-esteem.

Data from a cross national representative survey of black and white children (Dager and Thomas, 1986) aged seven through 11 years in single and two parent homes were used to assess the influence of certain mechanisms of socialization and family functioning variables on children's self-esteem. Results of multivariate analyses indicate that perceptions of neglect are critically associated with self-esteem for all cases. The variance in perceptions of neglect were related to problems in family functioning, for example, lack of helping responsibilities, intermittent mother absence, low levels of family interaction, over-permissiveness in rule enforcement, and parent-child argument.

Much research has postulated that single parent families contribute to delinquency, psychological, and learning problems among children. These problems could have been caused by the conflict in the family prior to the physical separation of the parents, or to the ensuing lowered socioeconomic status of most single parent families. When families that depict the population of interest more precisely are studied, especially when the socioeconomic status is controlled, the differences in child outcomes (delinquency, psychosocial, and learning problems) due to family structure disappear (Raschke and Raschke, 1979).

Feldman and Feldman (1979) compared younger children in different family structures and did not find the single parent families to have adverse effects for their adjustment or developmental characteristics. In an extensive review of the literature on fatherless homes covering 20 years, Feldman and Feldman (1979) concluded that there was little reliable evidence to support the charge that being reared in a mother headed family is detrimental to the child. In a review of these studies related to juvenile delinquency, they found that family quality, harmony, or climate have a stronger relationship with juvenile delinquency. They also found that discord and conflict in the two-parent home can be more detrimental to the child than father absence in the one-parent home.

Family conflict has been associated with inconsistent parenting, increased punitiveness, decreased use of reasoning as a discipline strategy, and fewer parental rewards (Stoneman, Brody, and Burke, 1989). Single mothers may be at particularly high risk, due partly to associated stressors of financial needs and the lack of support from a spouse (Webster-Stratton, Kolpacoff, and Hollinsworth, 1989). Raschke and Raschke (1979) found that the more children perceived the presence of conflict within their families, the lower the self-concept of children in single-parent families and intact families.

SELF-CONCEPT AND ITS RELATION TO BEHAVIORAL PROBLEMS

A child's inner feelings about himself are often the root cause of many difficulties. His inner self may rebel against loved ones, school, rules, and routines - all because he feels inadequate, unloved, stupid or ugly. These oppositional behaviors usually manifest themselves in two ways; a feeling of inability to cope with the world or the feeling of being unlovable (Yawkey, 1973). Children's behavior and the way in which they speak about themselves provide others with information about how they view themselves. Kindergarten children with a positive self-concept are described as unafraid of new situations, making friends easily, experimenting with new materials, trusting their teachers, being cooperative and able to follow reasonable rules, assuming responsibility for their behavior, being independent, and enjoying life. Children with low self-concept, on the other hand, rely on others for direction, ask permission to do anything, seldom show spontaneity or initiative, rarely attempt new activities, isolate themselves from others, rarely talk, are possessive of objects, and withdrawn or aggressive (Yawkey, 1973). Children with positive self-concept tend to view themselves as capable individuals. Therefore, they approach their surroundings with open questions, motivated to explore new opportunities and try challenging activities that will expand the limits of their understanding.

Research has been conducted which examines the relation between children's behavioral problems and parenting behavior. In a study that looked at toddlers' pretend play and autonomy development, mothers who reported higher levels of stress within areas of life related to parental adjustment (i.e. relationship with spouse, social isolation, health) had toddlers who exhibited more externalizing and total child behavioral problems. In addition, mothers who reported higher levels of stress in relation to their toddler were more likely to have toddlers who exhibited child behavior problems, less pretend play, and less usage of self-assertion during home observations. Fathers of toddlers who reported higher levels of stress in relation to their toddler also reported more behavioral problems (Creasey and Jarvis, 1994).

Significant correlations were consistently found between child behavior ratings and maternal depressive symptoms, social support, and life stress by Leadbeater and Bishop (1994). Direct associations between maternal stress, maternal guilt and anxiety, and dramatic and functional play have been found by Roopnavine, Church, and Levy (1990). Mother's marital companionships also showed direct associations with solitary and functional play among three to four year old children (Roopnavine, et al., 1990).

Specific to the homeless population, fairly similar results have been found. Dadds, Braddock, Cuers, and Elliot (1993) compared 51 female and 68 male homeless adolescents to 73 female and 51 male non-homeless youths (all subjects aged 13-18 years) in Australia on the self-reported incidences of personal and family problems. The homeless subjects reported the highest incidence of all behavioral and emotional problems, parental marital discord, and the lowest levels of parental care and acceptance.

CONCLUSION

If a child is to achieve a healthy self-concept all components of his being must be challenged and developed. Intelligence, physical skills, socialization techniques, or emotional control alone will not make a happy, healthy child. All facets of a child's functioning must be adequately developed, and they must work in unison.

A child's self-concept is affected by many variables, but none is as important as the self-concept and self-esteem of the parents (Sullivan, 1945; Killeen, 1993). Parents provide the model for self-acceptance and the feelings that life is worthwhile and "I can do it." Also, parents who demonstrate a positive self-concept and high self-esteem treat their children with respect and acceptance and provide them with encouragement and support. Parents who are struggling with their own self-worth, poverty, minimal education, and limited employment skills, like the homeless, are at high risk of failing to have such relationships with their children.

Chapter V

Research Design and Methodology

This study is a comparative study of two distinct groups of families — currently homeless and housed low-income. The purpose of the study was to examine the differences in process resources in both groups of families and the differences in the psychological well-being of the children of both groups of families. The study also examined the relationship between families' process resources and children's psychological well-being.

Process resources were measured in four areas: social support, interpersonal relationships within the family, personal growth within the family, and parenting quality. The children's psychological well-being was measured by using two variables: self-concept and behavioral problems.

Qualitative data were also gathered from the parents and children five years and older. All parents and children were asked the same questions (See Appendices N and O), and prevailing themes were drawn from the information gathered from homeless parents, housed parents, homeless children, and housed children separately.

The research design and methodology is that of small group administration of questionnaires to parents and individual administration to children.

The hypotheses of the study are as follows:

(1) Homeless families have less informal support, formal support, perceived support, and social embeddedness than housed low-income families.

(2) Homeless families have poorer interpersonal relationships than housed low-income families.

(3) Homeless families reflect less personal growth than housed low-income families.

(4) Homeless parents have poorer parenting quality than housed low-income parents.

(5) Homeless children have poorer self-concept than housed low-income children.

(6) Homeless children have more behavioral problems than housed low-income children.

(7) There are positive correlations among personal growth, interpersonal relationships, and parenting quality and children's self-concept within both groups of families.

(8) There are negative correlations among parenting quality, interpersonal relationships, and personal growth and children's behavioral problems within both groups of families.

The data was analyzed by computing: (1) Means and standard deviations of demographic data; (2) Chi Squares on demographic data and, categorical variables to test for significant differences between homeless and housed mothers and children; (3) t-tests to determine if homeless families have lower process resources (less social support, poorer interpersonal relationships, lower personal growth features, and poorer parenting quality) than housed low-income families; (4) 2-way ANOVAS - 2(housing status) x 2(gender of child), and Chi Squares to determine if homeless children have compromised psychological well-beings (poorer self-concept, and more behavioral problems) than housed low-income children; (5) bivariate correlations between interpersonal relationships and self-concept, personal growth and self-concept, parenting quality and self-concept, and parenting quality and behavioral problems; and (5) nonhierarchical multiple regression to determine the strongest predictors of self-concept and behavioral problems among the process resources. See Table 1.

PARTICIPANTS

Participants in the homeless group were drawn from shelters and motels for homeless families from a large metropolitan area. All homeless participants were screened to ensure that all were homeless and were residing in shelters. The housed low-income families were recruited from Social Services offices and an elementary public school located in a very low-income area. The housed families were screened to ensure that they were actually low-income; that is, a recipient of public entitlement(s), Head Start participant or school lunch program participant.

The children ranged from ages four through eight years. The children participating in the study were screened to ensure that they were all residing with their parents. See Appendices F and G for participant screening sheets. The study included only one child, either male or female, within the age range of four through eight from each participating family. Therefore, if a family had more than one child between the age of four and eight, only one child participated. The determination of which child participated in the study was made through random selection.

Table 1. Hypotheses and the Corresponding Analytic Plan

HYPOTHESES	ANALYTIC PLAN
HYPOTHESES 1-3 Homeless families have less process resources (interpersonal relationships, personal growth, parenting quality, and social support) than housed low-income families	1. t-tests
HYPOTHESES 4-5 Homeless children have more compromised psychological well-beings (poorer self-concept and more behavioral problems) than housed low-income children.	1. 2-Way ANOVA 2. Chi Squares
HYPOTHESES 6 There are positive correlations among personal growth, interpersonal relationships and parenting quality and children's self-concept.	1. Bivariate Correlation
HYPOTHESIS 7 There are negative correlations among behavioral problems and parenting quality, interpersonal relationships, and personal growth.	1. Bivariate Correlation
Exploratory — to identify the strongest predictors of children's psychological well-being (self-concept and behavioral problems)	1. Nonhierarchical Multiple Regression

Seventy-four homeless parent-child dyads and 74 housed parent-child dyads participated in the study. Sample size of the study is selected to provide a power of 80% or higher to detect medium sized effects in the analysis of the data (Cohen, 1977). Approximately 70 respondents per group is required to meet the 80% power to detect 88% variance between the two groups in a dichotomous independent measure, using a two-tailed test with alpha of .05.

MEASURES

Family Support Scale (FSS)

The FSS (Dunst, Jenkins, and Trivette, 1984) assesses enacted support, one of the two social support concepts described by Barrera (1986). The FSS is an 18-item questionnaire that is used to quantitatively measure the support available to mothers rearing young children (See Appendix H). Parents were asked to rate how helpful specific people are, for example their parents or professional groups, in raising their children. The alternatives for response fall on a five point lickert scale to include: (".") not applicable; (0) not at all helpful; (1) sometimes helpful; (2) generally helpful; (3) very helpful; and (4) extremely helpful.

To assist the mothers in choosing the appropriate responses, they were given a card listing the six alternatives. The question: "In the last three to six months, how helpful was each in raising your child?" was read to the respondents before the items were read. After the interviewer read each of the 18 items, the mothers were instructed to say the number corresponding to the choice that best answers the question. The interviewer then recorded the number response in the space provided on the questionnaire.

To score the responses, the items were grouped according to five subcategories, each containing several items, to include: formal kinship (parents, partner, partner's parents, relatives/kin, partner's relatives/kin, and children); informal kinship (friends, partner's friends, other parents, and co-workers); social group (church, social groups/clubs, and parents, and parent groups); professionals (family/child's doctor, professional help); and professional groups (school/day care, professional agencies, and Head Start). Indices of helpfulness were computed by summing the ratings of items within the five subcategories. The number of items per subcategory are not equal, therefore, each subcategory score was divided by the number of items in the subcategory, and then added to ten, a constant suggested by Dunst and Trivette (1986).

In addition, to the five subcategories, informal support and formal support subscales were computed. The informal support subscale includes the subcategories of formal kinship, informal kinship, and social groups. The formal support subscale comprises the remaining two subcategories (professionals and professional groups). Dividing the number of items in each subscale and adding ten also standardized the informal and formal support subscales. The total FSS score (referred to as the total enacted support score), which falls within a range of zero to 72, was calculated by summing the scores of all 18 items.

The FSS is reported to have internal consistency, a coefficient alpha of .84 for informal support and .87 for formal support for the population of this study. Cronbach's coefficient alpha for the entire scale was .79

Letiecq et al. (1996) conducted another test of internal consistency to ensure that the FSS was indeed a reliable measure of enacted support for a considerably different sample of respondents — low income, single, predominantly African American respondents, half of whom were homeless. Similar to the findings of Dunst et al. (1984), the FSS was found to have internal consistency (Cronbach's coefficient alpha was .81). In addition, internal consistency was found for the two subscales, informal support and formal support, with Cronbach's coefficient alpha of .78 and .70, respectively. The sample that Dunst et al. (1984) used to test the FSS consisted of predominantly married parents and the racial/ethnic make-up of the sample was not mentioned.

Social Embeddedness Questionnaire (SEQ)

The SEQ (Letiecq et al., 1996) is a simple four-item tool that asks for the number of people who are available to the respondent in times of need. This questionnaire measures social embeddedness and perceived social support (See Appendix I). The internal consistency (Cronbach's coefficient alpha) was .85 for the population of this study. Internal consistency was found for the two subscales, perceived support and embedded support, with Cronbach's coefficient alpha of .84 and .89, respectively.

Family Environment Scale (FES)

The FES (Moos and Moos, 1981) was designed to systematically assess the social or interpersonal climate of families. The FES is a 90-item, true or false, questionnaire that assesses the social environment characteristics of all types of families. It is composed of 10 subscales that assess three underlying dimensions: interpersonal relationships dimension (cohesion, expressiveness and conflict), personal growth dimension within the family (independence, achievement orientation, intellectual cultural orientation, active recreational orientation, and moral relationship emphasis), and systematic dimension (organization and control). See Appendix J. This study focused on two dimensions of the scale — interpersonal relationships and personal growth. However, the entire instrument was administered.

The FES has three forms: the Real Form (Form R), which measures existing perceptions of the family environment; the Ideal Form (Form I), which measures conceptions of ideal family environment; and the Expectation Form (Form E), which measures people's expectations of a new family environment (i.e. foster family) following a major family life cycle event. The Real Form was used in this study.

The FES has been standardized and normed on a sample of 1,125 normal and 500 distressed families. The normal sample included both single parent and multigenerational families from several ethnic minorities in various stages of the family life cycle and from several geographic sections of the United States.

The two dimensions of the FES that was used in this study, relationship dimension and personal growth dimension, had Cronbach coefficient alphas of .76 and .73, respectively.

The criterion validity of the FES has been established in more than 200 studies in which it has been found to discriminate normal from disturbed families, to differentiate family types, and to relate to treatment outcomes in predictable ways (Moos, Clayton, and Max, 1979; Moos and Spinard, 1984). Further studies corroborate these research findings, with the FES differentiating the families of socially maladjusted adolescence (Fox, Rotation, Macklin, Green and Fox, 1983).

In administering the FES the responses were marked on the question sheet then later transcribed onto the answer sheets to facilitate scoring. A set of standardized instructions was read to the respondents before the administration of the questionnaire (See Appendix K).

The items were arranged on the score sheet so that each column of responses on the answer sheet constitutes one subscale. To determine the raw score the number of Xs shown on the score sheet in each column was totaled. To determine the mean raw score for each subscale, the subscale raw scores were averaged. The form R Raw Score to Standardized Score Conversion Table (Moos and Moos, 1994) was used to convert raw scores to standard scores.

Parenting Dimensions Inventory (PDI)

The PDI (Power, 1989) is a 26-item instrument that measures nine parenting dimensions categorized into three subscales. The three subscales: (1) Support — (i) nurturance, (ii) sensitivity, (iii) nonrestrictive attitude; (2) Control — (iv) type of control (v) amount of control, (vi) maturity demands; and (3) Structure — (vii) consistency, (viii) organization; (ix) involvement. Parental support is the parents' ability to make the child feel comfortable, accepted, and approved (Thomas, Gecas, Weigert and Rooney, 1974). Parental control focuses on the amount of authority the parent exerts over the child, and includes such variables as discipline and punishment. The third construct, parental structure constitutes parental involvement and efforts in providing consistency and organization in the child's environment (Slater and Power, 1987). See Figure 4 and Appendix K.

The subscales of the PDI were first identified through confirmatory factor analysis with two primarily white, middle class samples (Slater and Power, 1987). The validity of the PDI was later confirmed with low-income, urban, African-American mothers (Kelley, Power and Wimbush, 1992).

The PDI is a multidimensional paper-and-pencil instrument developed from existing parenting assessment devices, which had published reliability and validity data. PDI items were drawn from existing instruments. Final scale items were selected through factor analysis to verify the subscales, after administration to 112 parents with at least one child between the ages of four and 14.

Cronbach's alpha coefficient for the population of this study for the three subscales, support, control, and structure were .72, .78, and .76, respectively.

To score the PDI the responses to the items that comprise each of the four subscales were averaged after the items that were scaled in a negative direction were reversed.

Research Design and Methodology 37

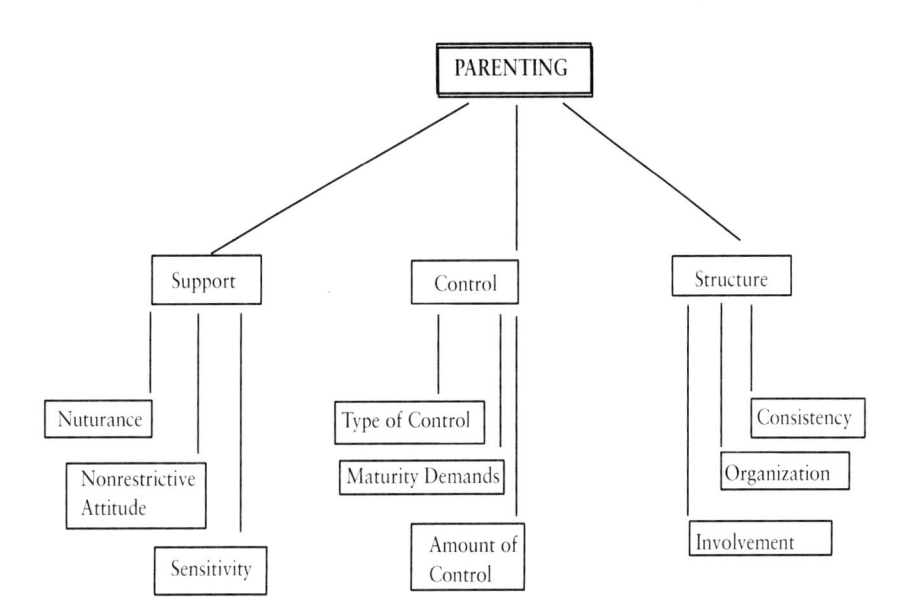

Figure 4. Multidimensional Parenting Model

```
                        PARENTING
              ┌─────────────┼─────────────┐
           Support        Control       Structure
           ┌──┴──┐        ┌──┴──┐        ┌──┴──┐
        Nuturance    Type of Control   Consistency
        Nonrestrictive  Maturity Demands  Organization
        Attitude
        Sensitivity    Amount of        Involvement
                       Control
```

Child Behavior Checklist (CBCL)

The CBCL (Achenbach and Edelbrock, 1983) is designed to be filled out by parents (and parent surrogate) under the assumption that they are typically among the most important sources of data about the children's competencies and problems. The checklist can be self-administered and it can be administered by an interviewer. For the purpose of this study the CBCL was administered by an interviewer. A copy of the questionnaire was given to the parent for her to follow along and the interviewer retained a copy. Before beginning with the interview, the interviewer said, "I'll read you the questions on this form and I'll write down your answers."

The CBCL measures two types of behaviors — competence and problem behaviors. This study measured problem behaviors only. The problem items, a total of 118, are responded to on a three point scale — (0) "Not True", (1) "Somewhat" or "Sometimes True", and (2) "Very True" or "Very Often". See Appendix L.

Cronbach's alpha coefficient for internalizing and externalizing behaviors subscales were .82 and .86, respectively.

Regarding the scoring of the CBCL, each item had a response zero, one, or two. To obtain the total raw score for each syndrome, the zeros, ones, and twos were entered on the scale and were added up. To compute the total problem score, the ones and the twos on the CBCL were summed up.

The total problem score was crosschecked by subtracting the number of items scored as present from the sum of ones and twos. A t-score for each problem score is provided by Achenbach (1991).

Piers-Harris Children's Self-concept Scale (CSCS) (The Way I Feel About Myself)

The CSCS (Piers and Harris, 1969) consists of 80 first-person simply written declarative statements, phrased positively or negatively, for example: "I am a happy person"; "It is hard for me to make friends"; "I wish I were different"; "I am good in my schoolwork". The response is "yes" or "no" to each item. The items are declarative sentences, half of them worded to indicate a positive self-concept and slightly more than half to indicate a negative self-concept. Negative terms such as "don't" are avoided because they can be confusing to young children (See Appendix M).

The scale was standardized on 1,183 children in grades 4 through 12, however, when the items are read by the examiner, children below grade three can take the test. Caution was taken to ensure that the scale does not correlate unduly with social desirability, and reasonable success was achieved. However, the correlations were quite high; -.54 to -.69 with a measure of anxiety. The authors believe this correlation represents a true trait correlation rather than one of response style. Therefore, the scale possesses sufficient reliability and validity to be used in research, as recommended by the authors.

Cronbach's alphas for children aged seven and eight of the population of this study for the specific dimensions of the self-concept measure were as follows: behavior, .79; intellectual and school status, .81; physical appearance and attributes, .88; anxiety, .84; popularity, .76; happiness and satisfaction, .78.

Items are scored in the direction of positive self-concepts so that the higher the raw score; the more positive the child's assessed self-concept. Total raw score is the total number of responses marked in the positive direction. To determine this score, the number of positive responses was totaled. Table 2 depicts the variables that each instrument measured.

PROCEDURES

This researcher contacted the directors of the targeted shelters for approval to conduct the study at the identified program sites. Contact for approval was made with the Chief of Emergency Services of the identified Department of Social Services (DSS), Department of Human Services (DHS), and the principal of the targeted elementary school. This researcher forwarded a brief description of the study to the homeless services directors and the Chiefs of Emergency Services. See Appendix A. Upon the approval from the program directors this researcher forwarded a one sheet document which describes the study and statements of solicitation for the participation of the residents to the homeless services program directors (See Appendix B). Personal visits were also made to the shelters to solicit resident participation.

After approval was acquired from the Chief of Emergency Services at the DSS and DHS sites, selected emergency services staff was assigned to assist with the selection of participants in the study. Copies of the one page summary/description of the study were forwarded to the selected staff. The selected staff then described the study to recipients of Aid to Families with Dependent Children (AFDC) and other entitlements and solicited their participation in the study.

A list of those who agreed to participate in the study was provided to this researcher who then coordinated interview sessions with them. With the approval of the Chief of Emergency Services, this researcher also directly approached families who came to the DSS and DHS offices to solicit their participation. The housed participants signed a consent form immediately before the beginning of each interview.

Request for Research Participants flyers (Appendix B) were handed out at the targeted elementary school to parents as they drop off and pick up their children. Fliers were also sent home with children. All interviews with parents and children were conducted in the school psychologist's office at the school.

Consent forms were forwarded to the shelters and a list of the participating residents was developed from the signed consent forms. See Appendix C. The staff who were assigned by the shelter director to work with this researcher coordinated the distribution and collection of the consent forms. Parents were also informed that their names would not be used on any materials for the study but that they needed to place their names on the consent form so that this researcher can know whom to pursue for interviews. Upon the receipt of the consent forms each parent and her child were assigned a participant number to ensure confidentiality. The participant number, and not their names, was used on all documents, except the consent form.

Each parent was administered the FSS, FES, PDI, and CBCL. The children were administered the Piers-Harris-CSCS.

The Piers-Harris-CSCS was administered to the older four year olds (four and a half and older) through eight year olds. However, data from the Piers-Harris-CSCS was only analyzed for children seven and eight years of age. The four year olds required much explanation and almost all required a break before completion of the interview. Approximately 4% of the five year olds were unable to complete the Piers-Harris-CSCS. All the children in this 4% were suspected to be hyperactive or immature for their age. All other five year olds were able to complete the Piers-Harris-CSCS without problems and a small percentage required a break.

Table 2. Instruments and the Variable Measured by Each One

INSTRUMENTS	VARIABLES MEASURED
1. The Family Environment Scale (FES)	1. Interpersonal Relation Dimension 　• cohesion 　• expressiveness 2. Personal Growth Dimension 　• Independence 　• Achievement orientation 　• Intellectual cultural orientation 　• Active recreational orientation 　• Moral relationship emphasis
2. Parenting Dimensions Inventory (PDI)	PARENTING QUALITY 1. Support 　• Nurturance 　• Nonrestrictive Attitude 　• Sensitivity 2. Control 　• Type of Control 　• Maturity Demands 　• Amount of Control 3. Structure 　• Consistency 　• Organization 　• Involvement
3. Family Support Scale (FSS) 4. Social Embeddedness Questionnaire (SEQ)	1. Informal and formal support 2. Perceived support and social embeddedness
5. Child Behavior Checklist (CBCL)	The behavioral patterns of children; competence and problem behaviors -- internal and external
6. Piers-Harris Children's Self-concept Scale (The Way I Feel About Myself)	The self-concept of children

　　Parent interviews were conducted in small groups of three to nine. All children interviews were done on an individual basis. There was no self-administered testing. Prior to administering the instruments standard introductions were read to all participants. See Appendix D and E. When administering the instruments, this researcher read the items to the participants and recorded the response given by the participant. This researcher met with the homeless participants in the shelters and motels in which they were residing and with the housed participants in the assigned rooms at the DSS and DHS sites or the school psychologist's office at the targeted school.

All the instruments (FES, FSS, SEQ, CBCL, PDI, the Piers-Harris-CSCS), and the qualitative questions took approximately 10 to 20 minutes each to administer. The total time for administration to adults was 45 minutes to an hour and 20 to 30 minutes for each child. All instruments were administered in one sitting. Participants did have the option to take a five-minute break, if needed. Adult participants were informed that they have the right to end the interview for themselves or their children at anytime they wish, and the children were told that if they did not want to answer any more questions they should inform the interviewer.

Chapter VI

Results

OVERVIEW

The results that follow are presented in two sections. Section one gives a description of the demographics of both groups of families and section two describes the functioning of homeless and housed families and children.

SECTION I — CHARACTERISTICS OF HOMELESS AND HOUSED FAMILIES

The homeless group included 74 parent-child dyads. Of the parents, 21 (28.38%) were 20 to 25 years; 29 (39.19%) were 26 to 30 years; 12 (16.22%) were 31 to 35 years; 8 (10.81%) were 36 to 40; and 4 (5.40%) were 41 to 45 years. All (100%) were African American. The greater proportion did not complete high school (45.9%); a smaller proportion completed high school or the General Equivalent Diploma (GED) (33.78%); and the least amount attended or graduated from college (20.27%). Almost three quarters (71.62%) were unemployed, 17.57% were employed part-time, and 10.81% were employed full-time. Half (50%) had been homeless for less than three months; a smaller percentage had been homeless for four to eight months (33.78%), 5.41% for nine to 12 months and 10.81% for longer than 12 months. More than half (52.70%) the group had lived in doubled-up housing in the past year and (47.30%) had not lived in doubled up housing in the past year.

The housed group included 74 parent-child dyads. Of the parents, 15 (20.27%) were between 20 and 25 years; 21 (28.38%) were 26 to 30 years; 19 (25.74%) were 31 to 35 years; 9 (12.10%) were 36 to 40 years; and 10 (13.51%) were 41 to 50 years. All (100%) were African American. Almost half (44.60%) did not complete high school, 29.73% either completed high school or the General Equivalent Diploma (GED) and 25.67% attended and/or graduated from college. More than half (62.16%) were unemployed; 10.81% were working part-time and 27.03% were working full-time. Approximately a quarter of them had lived in doubled-up housing in the past year (24.32%), and 60.81% had not been homeless in the past. See Table 3 for details on the age distribution and on other demographics.

Seventy-four homeless children were interviewed — 10 (13.51%) four year olds; 18 (24.32%) five year olds; 15 (20.27%) six year olds; 13 (17.57%) seven year olds; and 18 (24.32%) eight year olds. There were 34 (45.95%) males and 40 (54.05%) females, 7 (10.94%) children between five and eight years old were not enrolled in school, 57 (89.06%) were enrolled in school, 58 (90.63%) did not repeat any grades and six (9.37%) repeated grades.

Seventy-four housed children were interviewed. Their ages were as follows: 17 (22.97%) four year olds; 11 (14.87%) five year olds; 18 (24.32%) six year olds; 14 (18.92%) seven year olds; and 14 (18.92%) eight year olds. Thirty-eight (51.35%) were males and 36 (48.65%) were females. One (1.75%) child between five and eight years old was not attending school, 56 (98.25%) were attending school, and 51 (89.47%) had not repeated any grades while six (10.53%) had repeated grades.

Table 3. Parent Demographics

Variable	Homeless (N=74)	Housed (N=74)
AGE		
20-25	21(28.38%)	15(20.27%)
26-30	29(39.19%)	21(28.38%)
31-35	12(16.22%)	19(25.74%)
36-40	8(10.81%)	9(12.10%)
41-45	4(5.40%)	10(13.51%)
EDUCATION		
< High School	34 (45.95%)	33 (44.60%)
High School/GED	25 (33.78%)	22 (29.73%)
College	15 (20.27%)	19 (25.67%)
EMPLOYMENT		
No	53 (71.62%)	46 (62.16%)
Yes-part-time	13 (17.57%)	8 (10.81%)
Yes-full-time	8 (10.81%)	20 (27.03%)
LENGTH OF HOMELESSNESS		
< 3 mths.	37 (50.00%)	--
4 to 8 mths.	25 (33.78%)	--
9 to 12 mths.	4 (5.41%)	--
> 12 mths.	8 (10.81%)	--
DOUBLED UP HOUSING		
No	35 (47.30%)	56 (75.68%)
Yes	39 (52.70%)	18 (24.32%)
PAST HOMELESSNESS		
No	--	45 (60.81%)
Yes	--	29 (39.19%)

Results

Table 4. Frequency Distribution — Child Demographics

Variable	Homeless (N=74)	Housed (N=74)
AGE		
4	10 (13.51%)	17 (23.97%)
5	18 (24.32%)	11 (14.87%)
6	15 (20.27%)	18 (24.32%)
7	13 (17.57%)	14 (18.92%)
8	18 (24.32%)	14 (18.92%)
GENDER		
Male	34 (45.95%)	38 (51.35%)
Female	40 (54.05%)	36 (48.65%)
ATTENDING SCHOOL	(n=64)	(n=57)
No	7 (10.94%)	1 (1.75%)
Yes	57 (89.06%)	56 (98.25%)
REPEATED GRADES	(n=64)	(n=57)
No	58 (90.63%)	51 (89.47%)
Yes	6 (9.37%)	6 (10.53%)

Table 5. Mean Ages of Parents and Children

Variable	Homeless (Parent N=74/Children N=74)		Housed (Parent N=74/Children N=74)	
	Mean	Std. Dev.	Mean	Std. Dev.
Parent age	29.30	6.00	31.46	6.88
Children age	6.15	1.39	5.96	1.43

Chi Squares were completed to determine if both groups of parents differed significantly on demographic data such as age, education, employment, and doubled up housing. There were significant differences between the groups on employment (c^2 (2, N=148)=6.83, p < .05) and doubled up housing (c^2 (2, N=148)=12.58, p < .05). Homeless families had a higher rate of unemployment and a higher rate of doubled up housing. See Table 6 for additional results from Chi Squares application.

Table 6. Results of Chi Squares Comparing Homeless and Housed Parents

Variable	Phi Coefficient	Pearson Chi Square	P-value
Age	.41	25.48	.55
Education	.07	.68	.71
Employment	.21	6.83	.03
Doubled up housing	-.29	12.58	.00

$p < .05$

Chi Squares were completed to detect significant differences among the children on age, gender, school attendance and repeated grades. There was no significant difference on age, gender, school attendance or repeated grades.

Table 7. Results of Chi Squares Comparing Homeless and Housed Children

Variable	Phi Coefficient	Pearson Chi Square	P-value
Age	.17	4.31	.36
Gender	-.05	.43	.51
School attendance	.19	4.19	.12
Repeated grades	.09	.93	.63

$p < .05$

SECTION II — THE FUNCTIONING OF HOUSED AND HOMELESS FAMILIES AND CHILDREN

FAMILY FUNCTIONING VARIABLES

T-tests were completed on all family functioning variables to determine if significant differences existed between the homeless and housed groups. Table 8 gives the mean, t-values, and 2-tail significance values for all family functioning variables.

Results

Table 8. Comparison of Means Among Family Functioning Variables

Variable	Homeless			Housed			df	t-Value	2-Tail Sig.
	N	Mean	SD	N	Mean	SD			
Formal Support	74	21.94	1.31	74	21.64	1.05	146	1.58	.12
Informal Support	74	21.14	.87	74	21.21	1.37	146	-.41	.68
Enacted Support	74	57.28	4.51	74	56.80	7.34	146	.48	.63
Perceived Support	74	7.03	4.87	74	10.85	5.14	146	-4.58	.00
Social Embeddedness	74	5.34	4.03	74	8.78	4.93	146	-4.59	.00
Personal Growth	74	49.01	7.10	74	51.93	5.56	146	-2.78	.01
Interpersonal Relationship	74	43.61	10.38	74	48.89	7.50	146	-3.54	.00
Parental Control	74	3.76	.74	74	3.94	.71	146	-1.53	.13
Parental Support	74	4.42	.89	74	4.37	.79	146	.33	.74
Parental Structure	74	4.05	.84	74	4.17	.88	146	-.81	.42
Total Parenting Quality	74	12.41	1.63	74	13.84	1.93	146	-1.02	.31

Hypothesis #1: Homeless families have less social support than housed low-income families.

There were significant differences between the homeless and housed groups on social embeddedness (p=.00, t=-4.59) and perceived support (p=.00, t=-4.58); homeless families (M=5.34) had less social embeddedness than housed families (M=8.78). Homeless families (M=7.03) also perceived significantly less social support than housed families (M=10.85).

Hypothesis #2: Homeless families have poorer interpersonal relationships than housed low-income families.

There was a significant difference between the two groups on the interpersonal relationships dimension of the FES (p=.001, t=-3.54). Homeless families (M=43.61) had poorer interpersonal relationships than housed families (M=48.89).

Hypotheses #3: Homeless families have less personal growth attributes than housed low-income families.

There was a significant difference between the two groups on the personal growth dimension of the FES (p=.006, t=2.78); homeless families (M=49.01) had less personal growth attributes than housed families (M=51.93). The personal growth level of homeless families fell within the low-average range (30 to 50) while the housed families' fell within the high-average range (50 to 70).

Hypothesis #4: Homeless families have poorer parenting quality than housed low-income families.
There were no significant differences between the two groups on any specific domain of parenting quality (parenting structure, parenting support, parenting control) or total parenting quality. The means of parental control and parental structure were lower for homeless families (parental control=3.76 and parental structure=4.05) than housed families (parental control=3.94 and parental structure=4.17). Total parenting quality was also lower for homeless families (12.41) than housed families (13.84).

CHILD OUTCOME VARIABLES

Following are the analyses conducted regarding child outcome variables. Two-way ANOVA procedures were conducted to determine the joint effects of gender and housing status on all child outcome variables. Secondly, Chi-Squares were conducted to determine if significant differences existed between the groups' ratings of behavioral problems (normal, borderline, clinical) and the ratings of self-concept domains (low, average, high).

Hypothesis #5: Homeless children have poorer self-concept than housed low-income children.
Analyses of the Piers-Harris-CSCS results were conducted on seven and eight year old children only because the Piers-Harris-CSCS was normed on children in grades three through twelve. However, the manual does state that the test can be administered to younger children if the items are read to them individually and the examiner records the responses. Table 9 gives the numbers and percentages of homeless and housed children who scored low, average, and high in the specific domains and in global self-concept. Tables 10 and 11 give the numbers and percentages of homeless and housed boys and girls who scored low, average, and high in the specific domains and in global self-concept as defined by the Piers-Harris-CSCS.

Housing Differences

More housed children (53.57%) reported higher anxiety self-concept (perceived themselves with little anxiety) than homeless children (34.48%). Less homeless children (29.03%) had higher behavior self-concept than housed children (50.00%). More homeless children had low intelligence self-concept than housed children (19.36% versus 14.29%) and more housed children had high intelligence self-concept than housed children (58.06% versus 78.57%). Less homeless children had high happiness self-concept than housed children (64.52% versus 71.42%). More homeless children had low popularity self-concept than housed children (32.26% versus 39.29%). Less homeless children had high global self-concept than housed children (22.58% versus 53.57%) and twice as many homeless chil-

Results 49

dren had low global self-concept than housed children (35.48% versus 17.86%).

Chi Squares (combined group—males and females) indicated a significant difference in the numbers of children with low, average, and high global self-concept (p=.01), with more homeless children falling in the low self-concept range. Chi Squares performed to detect differences between homeless and housed children revealed a significant difference in the numbers of girls with low, average, and high anxiety self-concept (p=.04), and global self-concept (p=.03). More homeless girls had low anxiety and global self-concept.

Two-way ANOVA (with gender and housing status as independent variables) indicated that the groups differed significantly on physical self-concept ($\underline{F}(148)=5.38,p=.02$); homeless children ($\underline{M}=9.48$) had lower physical self-concept than their domiciled peers ($\underline{M}=10.54$).

Table 9. Ratings of Homeless and Housed Children In Self-concept Domains

Self-concept Domain	Homeless (N=31)			Housed (N=28)		
	Low	Average	High	Low	Average	High
Anxiety	25.81% (n=8)	38.71% (n=12)	35.48% (n=11)	25.00% (n=7)	21.43% (n=6)	53.57% (n=15)
Behavior	19.36% (n=6)	51.61% (n=16)	29.03% (n=9)	10.71% (n=3)	39.29% (n=11	50.00% (n=14)
Happiness	12.90% (n=4)	22.58% (n=7)	64.52% (n=20)	14.29% (n=4)	14.29% (n=4)	71.42% (n=20)
Intelligence	19.36% (n=6)	22.58% (n=7)	58.06% (n=18)	14.29% (n=4)	7.14% (n=2)	78.57% (n=22)
Physical	12.90% (n=4)	9.68% (n=3)	77.42% (n=24)	10.71% (n=3)	10.71% (n=3)	78.58% (n=22)
Popularity	45.16% (n=14)	22.58% (n=7)	32.26% (n=10)	28.57% (n=8)	32.14% (n=9)	39.29% (n=11)
Global	35.48% (n=11)	41.94% (n=13)	22.58% (n=7)	17.86% (n=5)	28.57% (n=8)	53.57% (n=15)

More homeless boys had high anxiety (perceived themselves with little anxiety) (61.54% versus 53.33%), physical (92.31% versus 66.67%) and happiness (76.92% versus 66.67%) self-concept than housed boys. More housed boys had high behavior (40.00% versus 38.46%), intelligence (80.00% versus 61.54%), popularity (46.67% versus 38.46%) and global (60.00% versus 46.15%) self-concept than homeless boys.

More housed girls had high self-concept in all domains - anxiety (perceived themselves with little anxiety) (53.85% versus 16.67%); behavior (61.54% versus 22.22%); happiness (76.93% versus 55.56%); intelligence (76.93% versus 55.56%); physical (92.31% versus 66.67%); popularity (30.77% versus 22.22%); and global (46.16 versus 5.56%).

Gender Differences - Homeless Boys and Girls

More boys reported high anxiety self-concept (low perceived anxiety) than girls (61.54% versus 16.67%). No male had low happiness self-concept while 22.22% of the girls had low happiness self-concept. More boys had high happiness self-concept than girls (76.92% versus 55.56%). More boys had higher happiness (76.92% versus 55.56%), intelligence (61.54% versus 55.56%), physical (92.31% versus 66.67%), popularity (38.46% versus 22.22%), and global (46.15% versus 5.56%), self-concept than girls.

Table 10. Ratings of Homeless Boys and Girls in Self-concept Domains

Self-concept Domain	Boys (N=13)			Girls (N=18)		
	Low	Average	High	Low	Average	High
Anxiety	23.08% (n=3)	15.38% (n=2)	61.54% (n=8)	27.78% (n=5)	55.55% (n=10)	16.67% (n=3)
Behavior	15.34% (n=2)	46.15% (n=6)	38.46% (n=5)	22.22% (n=4)	55.56% (n=10	22.22% (n=4)
Happiness	0% (n=0)	23.08% (n=3)	76.92% (n=10)	22.22% (n=4)	22.22% (n=4)	55.56% (n=10)
Intelligence	15.38% (n=2)	23.08% (n=3)	61.54% (n=8)	22.22% (n=4)	22.22% (n=4)	55.56% (n=10)
Physical	7.69% (n=1)	0% (n=0)	92.31% (n=12)	22.22% (n=4)	11.11% (n=2)	66.67% (n=12)
Popularity	38.46% (n=5)	23.08% (n=3)	38.46% (n=5)	50.00% (n=9)	27.78% (n=5)	22.22% (n=4)
Global	38.46% (n=5)	15.39% (n=2)	46.15% (n=6)	33.33% (n=6)	61.11% (n=11)	5.56% (n=1)

Gender Differences – Housed Boys and Girls

There was no difference in the number of boys and girls who had high anxiety self-concept. More girls than boys had low anxiety self-concept (perceived themselves with high levels of anxiety). More girls than boys had high behavior (61.54% versus 40.00%), happiness (76.93% versus 66.67%), and physical (92.31% versus 66.67%) self-concept. More boys than girls had high intelligence (80.00% versus 76.93%), popularity (46.67% versus 30.77%) and global (60.00% versus 46.16%) self-concept.

Table 11. Ratings of Housed Boys and Girls in Self-concept Domains

Self-concept Domain	Boys (N=15)			Girls (N=13)		
	Low	Average	High	Low	Average	High
Anxiety	20.00% (n=3)	26.67% (n=4)	53.33% (n=8)	30.77% (n=4)	15.38% (n=2)	53.85% (n=7)
Behavior	13.33% (n=2)	46.67% (n=7)	40.00% (n=6)	7.69% (n=1)	30.77% (n=4)	61.54% (n=8)
Happiness	20.00% (n=3)	13.33% (n=2)	66.67% (n=10)	7.69% (n=1)	15.38% (n=2)	76.93% (n=10)
Intelligence	20.00% (n=3)	0% (n=0)	80.00% (n=12)	7.69% (n=1)	15.38% (n=2)	76.93% (n=10)
Physical	13.33% (n=2)	20.00% (n=3)	66.67% (n=10)	0% (n=0)	7.69% (n=1)	92.31% (n=12)
Popularity	40.00% (n=6)	13.33% (n=2)	46.67% (n=7)	15.38% (n=2)	53.85% (n=7)	30.77% (n=4)
Global	20.00% (n=3)	20.00% (n=3)	60.00% (n=9)	15.38% (n=2)	38.46% (n=5)	46.16% (n=6)

Hypothesis #6: Homeless children have more behavioral problems than housed low-income children.

Tables 12 and 13 give the numbers and percentages of homeless and housed boys and homeless and housed who fell in the normal, borderline and clinical range in behavioral problems.

More homeless girls had externalizing (25.00% versus 20.59%) and internalizing (10.00% versus 8.82%) behavioral problems in the clinical range than homeless boys. More homeless boys had total (29.41% versus 25.00%) behavioral problems in the clinical range.

Twice as many homeless boys had externalizing (20.59% versus 10.53%) and total behavioral problems (29.41% versus 13.16%) in the clinical range than housed boys. More then twice as many housed boys (18.42%) had internalizing behavioral problems than homeless boys (8.82%).

More homeless girls had externalizing (25.00% versus (11.43%); internalizing (10.00% versus 0%); and total (25.00% versus 14.29%) behavioral problems than housed girls.

Table 12. Ratings of Homeless and Housed Boys in Behavioral Problems

Behavioral Domain	Homeless (N=34)			Housed (N=38)		
	Normal	Borderline	Clinical	Normal	Borderline	Clinical
External	70.59% (n=24)	8.82% (n=3)	20.59% (n=7)	86.84% (n=33)	2.63% (n=1)	10.53% (n=4)
Internal	82.36% (n=28)	8.82% (n=3)	8.82% (n=3)	76.32% (n=29)	5.26% (n=2)	18.42% (n=7)
Total	70.59% (n=24)	0% (n=0)	29.41% (n=10)	73.68% (n=28)	13.16 (n=5)	13.16% (n=5)

Table 13. Ratings of Homeless and Housed Girls in Behavioral Problems

Behavioral Domain	Homeless (N=40)			Housed (N=35)		
	Normal	Borderline	Clinical	Normal	Borderline	Clinical
External	65.00% (n=26)	10.00% (n=4)	25.00% (n=10)	82.86% (n=29)	5.71% (n=2)	11.43% (n=4)
Internal	82.50% (n=33)	7.50% (n=3)	10.00% (n=4)	97.14% (n=34)	2.86 (n=1)	0% (n=0)
Total	65.00% (n=26)	10.00 (n=4)	25.00% (n=10)	80.00% (n=28)	5.71% (n=2)	14.29% (n=5)

Chi Squares analyses failed to reveal any significant differences between homeless and housed girls on any of the behavioral problem measures. The analyses did reveal that a significantly higher percentage of homeless than housed boys exhibited total behavioral problems at the clinical level (c^2 (2, N=147)=6.73, p<.05). When Chi Squares comparisons were made of the total groups of homeless versus housed children, results revealed a significant difference in the numbers of homeless and housed children falling in the normal, borderline, and clinical range in external behavioral problems (c^2 (2, N=147)=6.22, p<.05), with homeless children exhibiting more externalizing problems.

Homeless children also reflected significantly lower global self-concept- than housed children ((c^2(2,N=147)=8.54,p<.05). Additionally, significantly more homeless girls reflected low anxiety ((c^2(2,N=147)=6.40,p<.05) and global ((c^2(2,N=147)=7.20,p<.05) self-concept than housed girls.

Two way-ANOVA procedures (with gender and housing status as independent variables) indicated a significant interaction between gender and housing status (F (148)=3.937, p=.05) on internal behavioral problems. However, Scheffe post hoc tests revealed no significant differences between any of the four groups (homeless boys, homeless girls, housed boys, housed girls).

Table 14 summarizes the results of Chi Square analyses comparing the groups of children who received low, average, and high scores in the self-concept measure; and normal, borderline, and clinical scores on the CBCL. Tables 15 through 34 give the results of 2-Way ANOVA procedures for the child outcome measures.

Table 14. Chi Squares — Child Outcome Variables

HOMELESS AND HOUSED CHILDREN			
Variable	Phi-Coefficient	Pearson Chi Square	P-value
Global Self-concept	.38	8.54	.01
HOMELESS AND HOUSED GIRLS			
Anxiety	.45	6.40	.04
Global Self-concept	.48	7.20	.03
HOMELESS AND HOUSED CHILDREN			
External Behavioral Problems	.21	6.21	.04
HOMELESS AND HOUSED BOYS			
Total Behavioral Problems	.30	6.73	.03

Table 15. 2 x 2 ANOVA Table — Anxiety Self-concept

Homeless	Housed
\multicolumn{2}{c}{Boys}	
M = 9.00 SD = 3.76 N = 13	M = 9.87 SD = 3.44 N = 15
\multicolumn{2}{c}{Girls}	
M = 7.00 SD = 2.70 N = 18	M = 8.54 SD = 4.03 N = 13

Table 16. 2-Way ANOVA Table — Anxiety Self-concept

Source	df	Sum of Squares	Mean Square	F
Gender	1	40.12	40.12	3.37
Housing Status	1	20.95	20.95	1.76
Intrreaction	1	1.64	1.64	.14
Error	55	654.96	11.91	
Total	58	726.75	12.53	

Results

Table 17. 2 x 2 ANOVA Table — Behavior Self-concept

Homeless	Housed
Boys	
M = 11.85 SD = 3.05 N = 13	M = 12.27 SD = 3.15 N = 15
Girls	
M = 10.50 SD = 3.71 N = 18	M = 13.31 SD = 3.25 N = 13

Table 18. 2-Way ANOVA Table — Behavior Self-concept

Source	df	Sum of Squares	Mean Square	F
Gender	1	.34	.34	.03
Housing Status	1	37.75	37.75	3.39
Intreraction	1	20.64	20.64	1.86
Error	55	611.90	11.13	
Total	58	674.92	11.64	

Table 19. 2 x 2 ANOVA Table — Happiness Self-concept

Homeless	Housed
Boys	
M = 8.46 SD = 1.61 N = 13	M = 8.13 SD = 2.20 N = 15
Girls	
M = 7.22 SD = 2.34 N = 18	M = 8.61 SD = 1.56 N = 13

Table 20. 2-Way ANOVA Table — Happiness Self-concept

Source	df	Sum of Squares	Mean Square	F
Gender	1	2.08	2.08	.86
Housing Status	1	4.11	4.11	1.02
Interraction	1	10.73	10.73	2.67
Error	55	221.15	4.02	
Total	58	239.93	4.14	

Table 21. 2 x 2 ANOVA Table — Intelligence and School Status Self-concept

Homeless	Housed
\multicolumn{2}{c}{Boys}	
M = 12.00 SD = 5.00 N = 13	M = 13.40 SD = 5.05 N = 15
\multicolumn{2}{c}{Girls}	
M = 11.39 SD = 3.91 N = 18	M = 11.46 SD = 3.50 N = 13

Table 22. 2-Way ANOVA Table — Intelligence and school Status Self-concept

Source	df	Sum of Squares	Mean Square	F
Gender	1	1.09	1.09	.06
Housing Status	1	43.68	43.68	2.26
Intrreraction	1	1.64	1.64	.09
Error	55	1065.11	19.37	
Total	58	1114.75	19.22	

Table 23. 2 x 2 ANOVA Table — Physical Self-concept

Homeless	Housed
Boys	
M = 10.85 SD = 2.76 N = 13	M = 9.87 SD = 3.60 N = 15
Girls	
M = 8.50 SD = 3.55 N = 18	M = 11.31 SD = 1.89 N = 13

Table 24. 2-Way ANOVA Table — Physical Self-concept

Source	df	Sum of Squares	Mean Square	F
Gender	1	2.97	2.97	1.26
Housing Status	1	12.11	12.11	1.25
Interreaction	1	51.95	51.95	*5.38
Error	55	530.70	9.65	
Total	58	602.98	10.40	

Table 25. 2 x 2 ANOVA Table — Popularity Self-concept

Homeless	Housed
Boys	
M = 7.69 SD = 2.84 N = 13	M = 6.93 SD = 3.61 N = 15
Girls	
M = 6.06 SD = 2.53 N = 18	M = 7.46 SD = 2.40 N = 13

Table 26. 2-Way ANOVA Table — Popularity Self-concept

Source	df	Sum of Squares	Mean Square	F
Gender	1	4.45	4.45	.54
Housing Status	1	1.52	1.52	.18
Intreraction	1	16.98	16.98	2.04
Error	55	457.88	8.33	
Total	58	482.85	8.33	

Table 27. 2 x 2 ANOVA Table — Global Self-concept

Homeless	Housed
Boys	
M = 47.38 SD = 12.67 N = 13	M = 49.00 SD = 14.89 N = 15
Girls	
M = 40.44 SD = 10.97 N = 18	M = 49.15 SD = 12.20 N = 13

Table 28. 2-Way ANOVA Table — Global Self-concept

Source	df	Sum of Squares	Mean Square	F
Gender	1	166.82	166.82	1.04
Housing Status	1	386.14	386.14	2.40
Intrreaction	1	182.29	182.29	1.13
Error	55	8863.21	161.15	
Total	58	9707.73	167.38	

Table 29. 2 x 2 ANOVA Table — External Behavioral Problems

Homeless	Housed
Boys	
M = 12.41 SD = 8.85 N = 34	M = 11.10 SD = 8.05 N = 38
Girls	
M = 12.27 SD = 9.74 N = 40	M = 8.80 SD = 6.68 N = 35

Table 30. 2-Way ANOVA Table — External Behavioral Problems

Source	df	Sum of Squares	Mean Square	F
Gender	1	54.56	54.56	.77
Housing Status	1	209.18	209.18	2.93
Intreraction	1	43.02	43.02	.60
Error	143	10201.39	71.34	
Total	146	10499.40	71.91	

Table 31. 2 x 2 ANOVA Table — Internal Behavioral Problems

Homeless	Housed
Boys	
M = 5.76 SD = 5.62 N = 34	M = 6.60 SD = 5.40 N = 38
Girls	
M = 7.05 SD = 5.51 N = 40	M = 4.51 SD = 3.77 N = 35

Table 32. 2-Way ANOVA Table — Internal Behavioral Problems

Source	df	Sum of Squares	Mean Square	F
Gender	1	5.94	5.94	.22
Housing Status	1	26.29	26.29	.993
Intreraction	1	104.29	104.29	3.94
Error	143	3787.84	26.49	
Total	146	3924.83	26.88	

Results

Table 33. 2 x 2 ANOVA Table — Total Behavioral Problems

Homeless	Housed
Boys	
M = 30.38 SD = 21.24 N = 34	M = 29.92 SD = 19.04 N = 38
Girls	
M = 32.22 SD = 23.45 N = 40	M = 23.51 SD = 16.30 N = 35

Table 34. 2-Way ANOVA Table — Total Behavior Problems

Source	df	Sum of Squares	Mean Square	F
Gender	1	190.59	190.59	.464
Housing Status	1	769.69	769.69	1.87
Interreaction	1	622.63	622.63	*1.51
Error	143	58784.51	411.08	
Total	146	60348	413.35	

*p<.05

FAMILY FUNCTIONING VARIABLES AND CHILD OUTCOME VARIABLES

Bivariate correlations were conducted to determine how the family functioning variables related to the child outcome variables.

Hypothesis #7: There are positive correlations among personal growth, interpersonal relationships, and parenting quality and children's self-concept within both groups of families.

Hypothesis #8: There are negative correlations among parenting quality, interpersonal relationships, and personal growth and children's behavioral problems within both groups of families.

Correlations were completed within separate groups (homeless and housed). Tables 35 and 36 present the correlations for the homeless group and the housed group, respectively.

Homeless Children

There were significant negative correlations between anxiety self-concept and parental control ($r=-.33$); happiness self-concept and parental control ($r=-.28$); behavior self-concept and parental structure ($r=-.24$); and physical self-concept and parental structure ($r=-.24$). Results reveal that the higher parent control, the lower the children's anxiety self-concept (children perceive themselves as experiencing more anxiety). Higher parent control was also associated with lower self-concept in the happiness domain. The higher parental structure, the lower the children's behavior self-concept and physical self-concept.

There were no significant correlations among family functioning variables and behavioral outcome variables.

Housed Children

The significant correlations among the housed population were as follows: a positive correlation between personal growth and anxiety self-concept ($r=.54$); a positive correlation between personal growth and intelligence and school status self-concept ($r=.40$); a positive correlation between personal growth and global self-concept ($r=.44$); a positive correlation between personal growth and popularity self-concept ($r=.52$). a negative correlation between interpersonal relationships and anxiety self-concept ($r=-.44$); and a negative correlation between interpersonal relationships and behavior self-concept ($r=-.20$). Results indicate that the higher the personal growth strengths of the parents, the higher the children's self-concept with respect to anxiety self-concept, intelligence and school status, popularity self-concept, and global self-concept. Results also indicate that more interpersonal relationship strengths are associated with lower self-concept in the anxiety and behavior domains among the children.

Results

Significant correlations among child behavioral outcome variables and family functioning variables are as follows: a negative correlation between parental support and external behavioral problems (r=-.29); a negative correlation between interpersonal relationships and internal behavioral problems (r=-.24); a negative correlation between parental support and internal behavioral problems (r=-.25); and a negative correlation between parental support and total behavioral problems (r=-.28). Results indicate that more parental support is associated with fewer external, internal, and total behavioral problems. Results also indicate that more interpersonal relationship strengths are associated with fewer internal behavioral problems.

Table 35. Correlations — Homeless Population

Variables	1	2	3	4	5	6	7	8	9	10	11	12	13	14	15	16
1. Personal Growth	1.00	*.50	.05	.05	*.34	.20	.05	.11	.05	-.06	.03	.21	-.03	.06	.10	.04
2. Interpersonal Relationships	*.50	1.00	-.00	.08	.11	.08	.00	.05	-.04	.26	-.07	.08	.14	.08	.11	.09
3. Parenting Control	.05	-.00	1.00	*.23	.05	*.54	.02	.15	.04	-.33	-.06	-.28	-.11	-.19	-.12	-.22
4. Parenting Structure	.05	.08	*.23	1.00	.00	.62	.02	.16	.04	-.08	-.24	-.15	-.06	-.24	-.03	-.14
5. Parenting Support	*.34	.11	.05	.00	1.00	.46	-.12	-.12	-.14	.11	.10	.23	.14	-.04	.18	.12
6. Parental Quality Total	.20	.08	*.54	*.62	*.46	1.00	-.04	.11	-.03	-.31	-.04	-.15	-.07	-.22	-.21	-.21
7. Child Behavior (External)	.05	.00	.02	.02	-.12	-.04	1.00	*.53	*.90	-.09	-.08	-.30	-.38	*-.36	-.10	*-.36
8. Child Behavior (Internal)	.11	.05	.15	.16	-.12	.11	*.53	1.00	*.75	-.19	.04	-.02	-.15	-.17	-.14	-.13
9. Child Behavior (Total Score)	.05	-.04	.04	.04	-.14	-.03	*.90	*.75	1.00	-.19	-.09	-.23	-.36	-.32	-.12	-.34
10. Self-concept (Anxiety)	-.06	.26	-.33	-.08	.11	-.31	-.09	-.19	-.19	1.00	*.38	*.46	*.56	.18	*.78	*.72
11. Self-concept (Behavior)	.03	-.07	-.06	-.24	.10	-.04	-.08	.04	-.09	*.38	1.00	*.47	*.58	*.45	*.45	*.76
12. Self-concept (Happiness)	.21	.08	-.28	-.15	.23	-.15	-.30	-.02	-.23	*.46	*.47	1.00	*.50	*.72	*.43	*.73
13. Self-concept (Intelligence)	-.03	.14	-.11	-.06	.14	-.07	*-.38	-.15	*-.36	*.56	*.58	*.50	1.00	*.43	*.48	*.83
14. Self-concept (Physical)	.06	.08	-.19	-.24	-.04	-.22	*-.36	-.17	-.32	.18	*.45	*.72	*.43	1.00	.34	*.64
15. Self-concept (Popularity)	.10	.11	-.12	-.03	.18	-.21	-.10	-.14	-.12	*.78	*.45	*.43	*.48	.34	1.00	*.74
16. Self-concept (Global)	.04	.09	-.22	-.14	.12	-.21	*-.36	-.13	-.34	*.72	*.76	*.73	*.83	*.64	*.74	1.00

*p < .05

Results

Table 36. Correlations — Housed Population

Variables	1	2	3	4	5	6	7	8	9	10	11	12	13	14	15	16
1. Personal Growth	1.00	.17	.14	*.27	.05	-.07	.09	-.16	-.19	*.54	.23	.30	*.40	.27	*.52	*.44
2. Interpersonal Relationships	.17	1.00	*.30	*.35	*.34	.13	-.18	*-.24	-.19	*-.44	*-.20	-.24	-.15	-.08	-.17	-.33
3. Parenting Control	.14	*.30	1.00	*.47	*.24	.22	-.09	.05	-.04	-.07	-.09	-.24	-.05	-.28	-.21	-.22
4. Parenting Structure	*.27	*.35	*.47	1.00	*.28	.18	-.21	-.02	-.15	.19	-.07	-.06	.11	-.09	.11	.03
5. Parenting Support	.05	*.34	*.24	*.28	1.00	.16	*-.29	*-.25	*-.28	-.20	.18	.17	.07	.13	.01	.05
6. Total Parental Quality	-.07	.13	.22	.18	.16	1.00	-.01	.02	-.02	-.03	.01	-.05	.07	-.11	-.03	-.06
7. Child Behavior (External)	-.09	-.18	-.09	-.21	*-.29	-.01	1.00	*.56	*.88	-.25	-.33	-.37	-.29	*-.39	*-.42	*.41
8. Child Behavior (Internal)	-.16	*-.24	.05	-.02	*-.25	.02	*.56	1.00	*.83	-.26	*-.44	*-.39	-.33	*-.55	*-.49	*-.45
9. Child Behavior (Total Score)	-.19	-.19	-.04	-.15	*-.28	-.02	*.88	*.83	1.00	-.35	*-.41	*-.45	-.36	*-.51	*-.53	*-.48
10. Self-concept (Anxiety)	*.54	*-.44	-.07	.19	-.20	-.03	-.25	-.26	-.35	1.00	*.58	*.65	*.67	*.57	*.72	*.82
11. Self-concept (Behavior)	.23	*-.20	-.09	-.07	.18	.01	-.33	*-.44	*-.41	*.58	1.00	*.74	*.80	*.78	*.65	*.83
12. Self-concept (Happiness)	.30	-.24	-.24	-.06	.17	-.05	-.37	*-.39	*-.45	*.65	*.74	1.00	*.71	*.81	*.79	*.84
13. Self-concept (Intelligence)	*.40	-.15	-.05	.11	.07	.07	-.29	-.33	-.36	*.67	*.80	*.71	1.00	*.82	*.70	*.86
14. Self-concept (Physical)	.27	-.08	-.28	-.09	.13	-.11	*-.39	*-.55	*-.51	*.57	*.78	*.81	*.82	1.00	*.80	*.86
15. Self-concept (Popularity)	*.52	-.17	-.21	.11	.01	-.03	*-.42	*-.49	*-.53	*.72	*.65	*.79	*.70	*.80	1.00	*.86
16. Self-concept (Global)	*.44	-.33	-.22	.03	.05	-.06	*.41	*-.45	*-.48	*.82	*.83	*.84	*.86	*.86	*.86	1.00

*p < .05

EXPLORATORY ANALYSES

Nonhierarchical multiple regression was completed to determine the strongest predictors, among family process variables (personal growth, interpersonal relationships, parental control, parental structure, parental support, and total parental quality), of children's psychological well-being — behavioral problems (external, internal, and total score) and self-concept (behavior, intelligence and school status, anxiety, popularity, happiness, physical and global) within each group of families (homeless and housed). A separate analysis was done for each of the child outcome variables. Tables 37 through 46 present the results of the regression analyses, and are followed by a summary of significant findings.

Table 37. Multiple Regression Analyses for External Behavioral Problems

HOMELESS							
Predictor	df	Simple Correlation	F	P-Value	Root R^2 Increment	F	P-Value
Personal Growth	1	.049	.149	.709	.099	.659	.420
Interpersonal Relationships	1	.004	.000	.927	-.035	.083	.774
Parental Control	1	.024	.069	.887	.026	.047	.830
Parental Structure	1	.021	.031	.892	.020	.028	.869
Parental Support	1	-.115	.989	.158	-.102	.719	.399
Total Parental Quality	1	-.037	.001	.919	-.015	.016	.899
Residual	67	Mean Square = 91.515		Final R = .156		p = .945	
HOUSED							
Predictor	df	Simple Correlation	F	P-Value	Root R^2 Increment	F	P-Value
Personal Growth	1	.087	.018	.864	-.026	.045	.834
Interpersonal Relationships	1	-.185	2.423	.095	-.068	.306	.582
Parental Control	1	-.086	.008	.821	.047	.145	.705
Parental Structure	1	-.208	3.163	.057	-.120	.966	.329
Parental Support	1	-.289	.641	.247	-.228	3.610	.062
Total Parental Quality	1	-.008	.179	.691	.053	.184	.669
Residual	66	Mean Square =		Final R = .331		p = .246	

Results

Table 38. Multiple Regression Analyses for Internal Behavioral Problems

HOMELESS							
Predictor	df	Simple Correlation	F	P-Value	Root R^2 Increment	F	P-Value
Personal Growth	1	.108	.909	.084	.139	1.406	.240
Interpersonal Relationships	1	.046	.143	.692	-.025	.046	.830
Parental Control	1	.151	.024	.271	.009	.350	.556
Parental Structure	1	.158	1.167	.302	.056	.230	.633
Parental Support	1	-.117	1.085	.322	-.157	1.782	.186
Total Parental Quality	1	.113	.494	.120	.042	.125	.724
Residual	67	Mean Square = 31.065		Final R = .278		p = .473	
HOUSED							
Predictor	df	Simple Correlation	F	P-Value	Root R^2 Increment	F	P-Value
Personal Growth	1	-.169	2.200	.125	-.163	1.801	.184
Interpersonal Relationships	1	-.238	4.561	.044	-.192	2.515	.118
Parental Control	1	.047	.165	.172	.125	1.053	.309
Parental Structure	1	-.022	.034	.255	.080	.421	.519
Parental Support	1	-.247	5.080	.040	-.221	3.382	.070
Total Parental Quality	1	.019	.024	.834	.027	.047	.829
Residual	66	Mean Square = 21.450		Final R = .371		p = .122	

Table 39. Multiple Regression Analyses for Total Behavioral Problems

HOMELESS							
Predictor	df	Simple Correlation	F	P-Value	Root R^2 Increment	F	P-Value
Personal Growth	1	.055	.233	.731	.140	1.341	.251
Interpersonal Relationships	1	-.039	.114	.781	-.093	.585	.447
Parental Control	1	.035	.002	.927	.029	.055	.815
Parental Structure	1	.042	.125	.702	.035	.084	.773
Parental Support	1	-.142	1.551	.431	-.132	1.197	.278
Total Parental Quality	1	-.032	.068	.821	-.013	.012	.914
Residual	67	Mean Square = 519.975		Final R = .207		p = .805	
HOUSED							
Predictor	df	Simple Correlation	F	P-Value	Root R^2 Increment	F	P-Value
Personal Growth	1	-.191	2.873	.089	-.161	1.764	.189
Interpersonal Relationships	1	-.194	2.717	.084	-.088	.514	.476
Parental Control	1	-.038	.104	.689	.083	.458	.501
Parental Structure	1	-.150	1.538	.636	-.039	.102	.751
Parental Support	1	-.277	6.562	.001	-.233	.102	.751
Total Parental Quality	1	-.024	.038	.892	.055	.002	.967
Residual	66	Mean Square = 308.970		Final R = .347		p = .189	

Table 40. Multiple Regression Analyses for Anxiety Self-Concept

		\multicolumn{3}{c	}{HOMELESS}			
Predictor	df	Simple Correlation	F	P-Value	Root R² Increment	F	P-Value
Personal Growth	1	.042	.062	.857	-.174	.746	.396
Interpersonal Relationships	1	.245	1.691	.204	.345	2.826	.106
Parental Control	1	-.318	3.216	.042	-.285	2.117	.159
Parental Structure	1	-.065	.505	.444	.129	.404	.531
Parental Support	1	.164	3.203	.441	.313	2.608	.119
Total Parental Quality	1	-.291	4.208	.022	-.302	2.409	.134
Residual	24	Mean Square = 9.104		Final R = .571		p = .116	
		\multicolumn{3}{c	}{HOUSED}			
Predictor	df	Simple Correlation	F	P-Value	Root R² Increment	F	P-Value
Personal Growth	1	.544	12.706	.001	.576	10.930	.003
Interpersonal Relationships	1	-.445	12.852	.000	-.440	5.285	.031
Parental Control	1	-.073	.132	.960	-.178	.724	.404
Parental Support	1	-.203	1.056	.249	-.206	.970	.335
Total Parental Quality	1	-.031	.773	.341	.161	.585	.452
Residual	22	Mean Square = 8.105		Final R = .723		p = .004	

Table 41. Multiple Regression Analyses for Behavior Self-concept

		\multicolumn{3}{c	}{HOMELESS}			
Predictor	df	Simple Correlation	F	P-Value	Root R² Increment	F	P-Value
Personal Growth	1	.004	.000	.987	.120	.352	.559
Interpersonal Relationships	1	-.052	.067	.959	-.054	.071	.792
Parental Control	1	-.123	.383	.721	-.055	.073	.789
Parental Structure	1	-.265	2.329	.113	-.282	2.079	.162
Parental Support	1	.044	.051	.962	.103	.255	.618
Total Parental Quality	1	-.107	.281	.831	.023	.012	.913
Residual	24	Mean Square = 13.343		Final R=.332		p = .806	
		\multicolumn{3}{c	}{HOUSED}			
Predictor	df	Simple Correlation	F	P-Value	Root R² Increment	F	P-Value
Personal Growth	1	.232	1.587	.324	.271	1.750	.200
Interpersonal Relationships	1	-.196	1.100	.359	-.253	1.498	.234
Parental Control	1	-.086	.176	.646	.096	.203	.657
Parental Support	1	.178	.952	.509	.284	1.924	.179
Total Parental Quality	1	.009	.002	.509	-.157	.558	.463
Residual	22	Mean Square = 10.186		Final R = .424		p = .460	

Results

Table 42. Multiple Regression Analyses for Happiness Self-concept

			HOMELESS				
Predictor	df	Simple Correlation	F	P-Value	Root R^2 Increment	F	P-Value
Personal Growth	1	.197	1.247	.109	.294	2.277	.144
Interpersonal Relationships	1	.096	2.315	.113	.044	.046	.833
Parental Control	1	-.362	4.429	.032	-.368	3.760	.064
Parental Structure	1	-.163	.751	.393	-.177	.773	.338
Parental Support	1	.209	1.302	.372	.225	1.286	.268
Total Parental Quality	1	.203	.709	.399	-.136	.450	.509
Residual	24	Mean Square = 3.866		Final R = .563		p = .130	
			HOUSED				
Predictor	df	Simple Correlation	F	P-Value	Root R^2 Increment	F	P-Value
Personal Growth	1	.300	2.960	.123	.363	3.338	.081
Interpersonal Relationships	1	-.243	1.659	.207	-.246	1.416	.247
Parental Control	1	-.242	1.404	.228	-.097	.210	.652
Parental Support	1	.172	.805	.610	.223	1.147	.296
Total Parental Quality	1	-.054	.068	.623	-.063	.089	.769
Residual	22	Mean Square = 3.252		Final R = .523		p = .188	

Table 43. Multiple Regression Analyses for Intelligence and School Status Self-concept

			HOMELESS				
Predictor	df	Simple Correlation	F	P-Value	Root R^2 Increment	F	P-Value
Personal Growth	1	-.046	.057	.695	-.117	.331	.571
Interpersonal Relationships	1	.161	1.458	.220	.208	1.088	.307
Parental Control	1	-.163	.732	.450	-.140	.476	.497
Parental Structure	1	-.073	.131	.891	-.017	.007	.936
Parental Support	1	.105	.316	.729	.166	.679	.418
Total Parental Quality	1	-.111	.316	.568	-.064	.100	.755
Residual	24	Mean Square = 21.109		Final R = .317		p = .841	
			HOUSED				
Predictor	df	Simple Correlation	F	P-Value	Root R^2 Increment	F	P-Value
Personal Growth	1	.400	5.658	.031	.389	3.920	.060
Interpersonal Relationships	1	-.152	.585	.449	-.152	.518	.479
Parental Control	1	-.047	.053	.807	-.073	.118	.735
Parental Support	1	.072	.118	.729	.055	.066	.800
Total Parental Quality	1	.068	.102	.701	.021	.009	.924
Residual	22	Mean Square = 18.269		Final R = .452		p = .375	

Table 44. Multiple Regression Analyses for Physical Self-concept

HOMELESS							
Predictor	df	Simple Correlation	F	P-Value	Root R² Increment	F	P-Value
Personal Growth	1	.051	.779	.412	.205	1.051	.316
Interpersonal Relationships	1	.097	.251	.817	.102	.251	.621
Parental Control	1	-.243	1.733	.340	-.197	.972	.334
Parental Structure	1	-.253	1.855	.331	-.184	.837	.369
Parental Support	1	-.076	1.912	.327	-.045	.048	.829
Total Parental Quality	1	-.271	.316	.739	-.101	.246	.625
Residual	24	Mean Square = 12.031		Final R = .419		p = .567	
HOUSED							
Predictor	df	Simple Correlation	F	P-Value	Root R² Increment	F	P-Value
Personal Growth	1	.267	2.371	.134	.356	3.200	.087
Interpersonal Relationships	1	-.082	.050	.960	-.003	.000	.988
Parental Control	1	-.282	2.080	.120	-.153	.524	.477
Parental Support	1	.133	.448	.700	.145	.471	.500
Total Parental Quality	1	-.109	.013	.795	-.069	.104	.750
Residual	22	Mean Square = 8.458		Final R = .470		p = .320	

Table 45. Multiple Regression Analyses for Popularity Self-concept

HOMELESS							
Predictor	df	Simple Correlation	F	P-Value	Root R² Increment	F	P-Value
Personal Growth	1	.110	.301	.835	.042	.042	.839
Interpersonal Relationships	1	.100	2.451	.103	.024	.014	.908
Parental Control	1	-.108	.295	.739	-.039	.063	.851
Parental Structure	1	-.019	.009	.961	.056	.076	.785
Parental Support	1	.223	1.662	.224	.298	2.341	.139
Total Parental Quality	1	-.212	1.540	.241	-.313	2.608	.119
Residual	24	Mean Square = 7.765		Final R = .418		p = .545	
HOUSED							
Predictor	df	Simple Correlation	F	P-Value	Root R² Increment	F	P-Value
Personal Growth	1	.521	1.364	.239	.561	10.106	.004
Interpersonal Relationships	1	-.166	.638	.531	-.066	.095	.761
Parental Control	1	-.209	1.256	.240	-.288	1.994	.172
Parental Support	1	.015	.005	.889	-.066	.095	.761
Total Parental Quality	1	-.029	.020	.831	.103	.237	.631
Residual	22	Mean Square = 6.930		Final R = .632		p = .035	

Table 46. Multiple Regression Analyses for Global Self-concept

				HOMELESS			
Predictor	df	Simple Correlation	F	P- Value	Root R^2 Increment	F	P- Value
Personal Growth	1	.115	3.540	.056	.232	1.371	.253
Interpersonal Relationships	1	.016	.040	.807	-.032	.024	.878
Parental Control	1	-.239	1.717	.186	-.211	1.124	.300
Parental Structure	1	-.105	.269	.801	-.029	.020	.889
Parental Support	1	.003	.000	.899	.004	.000	.985
Total Parental Quality	1	-.221	1.316	.387	-.160	.634	.434
Residual		Mean Square = .628		Final R = .372		p = .696	
				HOUSED			
Predictor	df	Simple Correlation	F	P- Value	Root R^2 Increment	F	P- Value
Personal Growth	1	.406	6.216	.010	.442	5.327	.031
Interpersonal Relationships	1	-.243	1.536	.278	-.179	.728	.403
Parental Control	1	-.204	.049	.801	-.182	.755	.395
Parental Support	1	.008	.002	.878	.011	.003	.960
Total Parental Quality	1	-.063	.006	.837	.040	.035	.854
Residual	22	Mean Square = .533		Final R = .535		p = .161	

Homeless Families

There were no significant single or unique predictors of external, internal or total behavioral problems. All independent variables combined accounted for 2.43% of the variance in external behavioral problems, 7.73% for internal behavioral problems, and 4.28% for total behavioral problems.

Single significant predictors of anxiety self-concept were parental control (F=3.22, p=.04), which accounted for 10.41% of the variance, and parental support (F=3.20, p=.04) as a positive predictor, which accounted for 2.69% of the variance. Results indicated that parental control predicted children's lower self-concept in the anxiety domain. All the independent variables combined accounted for 32.60% of the variance in anxiety self-concept.

There were no significant single or unique predictors of behavior self-concept. All the independent variables combined accounted for 11.02% of the variance for behavior self-concept.

Parental control emerged as a single significant predictor of happiness self-concept (F=4.43, p=.03), accounting for 13.10% of the variance. Results indicated that parental control predicted children's lower self-concept in the happiness domain. All the independent variables combined accounted for 31.70% of the variance in happiness self-concept.

There were no significant single or unique predictors for intelligence and school status self-concept, physical self-concept, popularity self-concept, or global self-concept. All the independent variables combined accounted for 10.05% of the variance for intelligence and school status self-concept, 17.56% of the variance for physical self-concept, 17.47% of the variance for popularity self-concept, and 10.69% of the variance for global self-concept.

Housed Families

There were no significant single or unique predictors for external behavioral problems. All the independent variables combined accounted for 10.96% of the variance for external behavioral problems.

Interpersonal relationships (F=4.56, p=.044) and parental support (F=5.08, p=.040) were significant single predictors of internal behavioral problems, accounting for 5.66% and 6.10% of the variance, respectively. Results indicated that interpersonal relationship strengths and parental support predicted fewer internal behavioral problems. A combination of all the independent variables explained 13.76% of the variance.

Parental support (F=6.56, p=.00) was a significant single predictor of total behavioral problems accounting for 6.67% of the variance. Results indicated that parental support predicted fewer total behavioral problems. All the independent variables combined accounted for 12.04% of the variance.

Single predictors of anxiety self-concept were personal growth (F=12.71, p=.00) as a positive predictor, and interpersonal relationships (F=12.85, p=.00) as a negative predictor, accounting for 29.59% and 19.80% of the variance. Unique positive predictor was personal growth (F=10.93, p=.00) and interpersonal relationships (F=5.28, p=.03), accounting for 33.18% and 19.36% of the variance. Results indicated that personal growth predicted higher self-concept in the anxiety domain and interpersonal relationship strengths predicted lower self-concept in the anxiety domain. All the independent variables combined accounted for 52.27% of the variance.

There were no significant single or unique predictors for behavior self-concept or happiness self-concept. All the independent variables combined accounted for 17.98% of the variance for behavior self-concept and 27.35% of the variance for happiness self-concept.

Personal growth (F=5.66, p=.01) was a positive significant single predictor of intelligence and school status self-concept, accounting for 16.00% of the variance. Results indicated that personal growth predicted higher self-concept in the intelligence and school status domain. All the independent variables combined accounted for 20.30% of the variance.

There were no significant single or unique predictors for physical self-concept. All the independent variables combined accounted for 22.09% of the variance for physical self-concept.

Results

Personal growth (F=10.11, p=.00) was a significant single predictor of popularity self-concept, accounting for 7.62% of the variance. Results indicated that personal growth predicted higher self-concept in the popularity domain. All the independent variables combined accounted for 40.00% of the variance.

Personal growth (F=6.22, p=.01) was a significant single predictor of global self-concept, accounting for 16.48% of the variance. Personal growth also emerged as a unique positive significant predictor (F=5.33, p=.03), accounting for 19.54% of the variance. Results indicated that personal growth predicted higher global self-concept. All the independent variables combined accounted for 28.62% of the variance for global self-concept.

CHAPTER VII

Implications of Findings

This study examined the differences in family functioning variables (interpersonal relationships, personal growth, social support, and parental quality) among homeless and housed low-income families, and the differences between homeless and housed children's psychological well-being (behavioral problems and self-concept). Results show that homeless and housed families differed significantly on social embeddedness, and perceived support, with homeless families exhibiting less social embeddedness and less perceived support. Homeless families also showed significantly fewer personal growth attributes and poorer interpersonal relationships. The homeless and housed children differed significantly on measures of global and physical self-concept, with homeless children exhibiting poorer self-concept. Homeless children were significantly more likely to exhibit a high level of external behavioral problems than housed children. Homeless girls were more likely to exhibit low global and poorer anxiety self-concept than housed girls. Moreover, more homeless boys fell in the clinical range of external behavioral problems than housed boys.

In most cases where the difference between both groups of children by housing status or gender was not significant, there was noticeable difference between the groups. The homeless group often reflected less positive and more negative attributes. For example, homeless parents scored higher on control and lower on structure and total parental quality than housed families. More homeless children than housed children reported low anxiety (perceived themselves with high levels of anxiety), behavior, intelligence, happiness, popularity, and global self-concept.

The discussion that follows addresses the findings of the study and their implications for program development; public policies, and funding for homeless families. The subtle differences between homeless and housed low-income families that this study addresses are also brought into focus.

THE EFFECTS OF POVERTY COUPLED WITH HOMELESSNESS ON FAMILIES

Research has repeatedly shown that the two groups of families of this study (homeless and housed) are similar but are also different in specific domains (Bassuk and Rosenberg, 1988; Wagner and Pervine, 1994). Both groups of families live in poverty, an experience that has a myriad of consequences that are very similar for anyone who experiences it. Two common descriptors of families in poverty are low levels of education and high levels of unemployment. Similar to the findings of Bassuk and Rosenberg (1988), both groups of families in this study bore these descriptors. Both the homeless (45.95% had less than high school education) and the housed group (44.60% had less than high school education) had low levels of education, with no significant difference between them. Both the homeless (71.62% unemployed and 10.81% employed part-time) and the housed group (62.16% unemployed and 27.03% employed part-time) had high levels of unemployment, although the housed families were more likely to be employed full-time rather than part-time.

While the families are similar because of the common denominator of poverty, the homeless families do have unique experiences that are outcomes of their existing situation, a situation that is not shared by the housed families. As stated previously, more mothers of the homeless group were employed part-time, and this could be a function of the transitory nature of their residence or the structure and confines within which most homeless families reside. Most, if not all, shelters have strict rules about departure times from the shelter, the times residents can return, and curfew hours. Most family shelters do not provide childcare and do not allow for residents to care for other residents' children. Most shelters have chores assigned to each adult resident that must be completed by a certain time. Failure to comply with these rules results in termination or eviction of the family from the residence (Anderson and Koblinsky, 1995). These limitations and restrictions and the prevailing need to maintain shelter may contribute to the homeless parents' increased likelihood of unemployment. A low employment acquisition rate among the homeless was also found by Maza and Hall (1988). They found that as little as 7% married females, 17% married males, 11% single females and 6% single males found employment after becoming homeless.

The homeless group had significantly more children (five through eight years) who were not attending school than the housed group. This finding confirms that of Hall and Maza (1990) (Rafferty and Rollins, 1989) who reported that more homeless than domiciled children were not attending school. There are several reasons why homeless children are less likely to be attending school. A leading cause is assumed to be the instability and unpredictability in which homeless families live. Homeless mothers are also often times preoccupied with other issues such as submitting applications for public entitlement(s), rather than taking the necessary steps to enroll their children in school. Additionally, homeless children often suffer from asthma, upper respiratory infections, and diarrhea and they are often afflicted more frequently and more severely with common childhood illnesses such as ear infections and the common cold.

One of the theoretical bases upon which this study is built may help to explain the difference between the two groups in school attendance. Maslow (1954) considers physiological needs as the basic needs of the human species. These are needs that must be first adequately met before one can respond to the needs at the higher levels. It has been established that these basic needs are not adequately met for homeless families; therefore, the higher priority will be to fulfill the basic needs first. Setting academic and even housing goals of less importance than meeting daily basic need for food and shelter (Zeifert and Strauch-Brown, 1991).

Lower rates of school attendance among homeless children could be an explanation for higher rates of unemployment or higher rates of part-time employment. If children are not in schools and there is minimal social support, as reported by this and other studies (Dornbusch, 1994; Letiecq et al., 1996), then the mothers are forced to provide care. The transient nature of the lives of homeless families will also limit employment opportunities and retention. When compared to homeless families, housed families have more stability and significantly more social embeddedness (a finding of this study), and these immediately increase their chances for employment acquisition and retention, which compliment a family environment in which the children attend school. This is so because, if the mothers are working, the most realistic day-time care for school-aged children is school.

This study confirms the finding in the literature that doubled-up housing precedes homelessness (Weitzman et al., 1990). More than half of the homeless families had lived in doubled-up housing in the past year. If doubled-up housing is to be considered homelessness, which is the case in some contexts, then the length of homelessness reported by the participants would be even greater. Twenty-one percent of the housed had lived in doubled-up housing in the past year, a suggestion that both populations share some common characteristics-mainly lack of financial resources. In addition, thirty-six percent of the housed had been homeless in the past, another confirmation that both populations experience similar stressors.

SOCIAL SUPPORT

Contrary to the hypothesis that homeless families would exhibit less enacted support than housed families, both populations had low and relatively the same level of formal and informal support. There are a number of factors that may contribute to this finding. All the families who participated in the study were either Head Start participants, recipients of public benefits, or lunch program participants. All criteria for participating in this research are associated with formal support from Head Start staff, social services staff or other helping professionals. Both the homeless and the housed families have a small social network. Homeless mothers may be finding support in other mothers who reside in shelter with them. This finding is different from that of Boxill and Beaty (1987) who found that homeless mothers had no social support and tended to use their oldest child as their support system. However, the similarities in informal support reflect the resemblances in interpersonal relationships between both populations. Informal support taps into support received through interpersonal relationships, specifically from immediate family members, spouse, extended family, friends, coworkers, and social groups. The fact that both groups scored quite low, on a scale of zero to 72, and relatively the same in this domain may be an indication that they both have low personal ties and deficient interpersonal relationships.

Although there were no significant differences between homeless and housed families in enacted support, the differences between the two groups in this study on the quality of social support confirm prior evidence regarding homeless families' deficient interpersonal networks (Dornbusch, 1994; Letiecq et al., 1996). Social embeddedness measures the stability or durability of informal support, and perceived support measures how families view the support. The housed group had significantly more social embeddedness and perceived support than the homeless group. So although both the homeless and housed groups had relatively little actual informal support, whatever support the housed group had appeared more stable or consistent and more available to tap into in case of emergencies. This again could reflect the transient nature of homeless families. Due to their frequent moves they are less likely to establish and maintain informal support/relationships and there is insufficient time for them to develop the perception that there are other individuals they can rely on for assistance in times of need. Also, shelter rules and regulations (curfews; chores; meal times; limited phone use, if any; etc.) may increase social isolation from family and friends, reducing social embeddedness (Bassuk and Gallagher, 1990). Even though these restrictions exist, many homeless persons have a network of confidants, friends, relatives, and acquaintances. However, these ties differ somewhat from domiciled low-income families and do not satisfy most homeless individual's expressed need for support (Stark, 1994).

FAMILY PROCESSES

Poverty impacts families at various levels. One important area of impact is at the family functioning level, namely interpersonal relationships and personal growth. Families who reside in impoverished communities are exposed to violence and illicit drugs and are more prone to develop a sense of hopelessness or hostility (Bourgois, 1991) all of which will adversely affect family functioning. All the families of this study fell in the below average range in the personal growth and interpersonal relationships scales of the FES.

However, as confirmed by the findings of this study, the combination of poverty and homelessness appear to have a stronger negative impact on families than poverty alone. As hypothesized, homeless mothers exhibited greater problems with interpersonal relationships and significantly lower personal growth within the families than housed mothers.

Previous studies have found that homeless women, in comparison to their housed counterparts, have been found to have experienced higher rates of domestic violence and poorer interpersonal relationships (Hagan and Ivanoff, 1988), and higher rates of substance abuse and less meaningful relationships with men (Bassuk and Rosenberg, 1988). Poor families who come into shelter are not solely poor, but they may be coming from more deteriorated housing conditions and communities than most poor families, and they may have more social, medical and psychological challenges (Knickman and Weitzman, 1989). Therefore, the process resources of homeless families, in comparison to domiciled low-income families, may be lower.

The homeless group had poorer interpersonal relationships within their families than the housed group. This result supports the findings of Mills and Ota (1989) and Hagan and Ivanoff (1988) who found that one of two leading causes of homelessness is domestic violence (family dispute and poor interpersonal relationships). The lower level of expressiveness among the homeless families was expected because research shows that families often times lose their autonomy upon moving into shelters (Boxill and Beaty, 1987). Children often adhere to shelter rules rather than their parents', and heads of households respond to the demands of shelter authorities, some of which may conflict with the demands that exist within the individual families (Boxill and Beaty, 1987). In addition, families are forced to comply with shelter rules and policies, whether or not they agree with them, because failure to comply with these rules inevitably results in the termination of shelter services.

Personal growth, another family process variable, was also low for both groups of families. Poverty conditions negatively affect the psychological functioning of families (McLoyd, 1990), and both groups of families in this study reside in poverty. However, current results indicate that the homeless mothers exhibited significantly poorer personal growth within the family context than housed mothers. The homeless mothers' rating of significantly less personal growth within the family than the housed families supports the position that homelessness exacerbates the effects of poverty on families. Personal growth measures such dimensions as independence, achievement orientation, intellectual-cultural orientation, active-recreation orientation, and moral-religious emphasis. Emergency shelters are often described as "accommodative" responses to the housing needs of the

homeless (Snow and Anderson, 1993). Shelters replicate, on a limited and temporary basis, some of the basic functions of a home (Gounis, 1992). They provide facilities for sleeping, eating and bodily hygiene. While it should be possible to provide for these basic necessities in an informal and uncomplicated manner, this rarely occurs in our nation's shelters. Instead, in the process of "professionalization", homeless shelters have become increasingly institutionalized (Stark, 1994). Routine schedules, the constant supervision of families by staff, and the large number of occupants in one place limit autonomy, independence, individuality (either as a single individual or as a family), and recreation, cultural and religious activities as a family. The following quote depicts the general feelings of shelter residents and reflects why there may be limited aspiration toward personal growth:
"When you live in a shelter other people control your life. They tell you when you may come in and when you must go out. They tell you when you can take your shower and when you can wash your clothing." (Liebow, 1993, p. 121).

Seven themes emerged from a previous study in which shelter residents were interviewed (Bauman, 1993): (1) boundaries; (2) connections; (3) fatigue/despair; (4) self-respect; (5) lack of determination; (6) privacy; and (7) mobility. Boxill and Beaty (1987) coined the concept, "public mothering", which describes a setting of constant scrutiny within which homeless parents rear their children. Homeless parents disclose that a setting of this sort limits the sharing of their value systems with their children, and it suffocates autonomy and limits privacy. These features characterize shelter living; therefore the probability of reduced personal growth for homeless families may be higher.

PARENTING CAPACITY

Although homeless parents scored higher on parent control, lower on parent structure and lower on overall parenting quality, the results of this study revealed no significant difference in parenting quality between homeless and housed low-income parents. However, there was deficient parenting in both groups of parents as reflected in the scores from the PDI, a finding that supports McLoyd (1990) model of how poverty and economic loss affect children. Even housed parents have to contend with overwhelming stressors that permeate their lives and affect their capacity to parent in appropriate ways.

Poverty is one of the leading life circumstances that create a stressful parenting context and homelessness is an extreme expression of poverty. A context of daily hassles, like that of shelter living also provides for a stressful parenting context.

Homeless parents live under constant supervision and scrutiny by shelter staff. There is much structure and control within the shelters, therefore

Implications of Findings 83

the parents are forced to at least temporarily adjust their parenting quality, which may be improved because of the structure that family shelter programs provide. On the other hand, parenting quality may deteriorate because the rules and fear of eviction from the shelter cause parents to become overly controlling. Parents are monitored to ensure that the children are closely supervised, appropriately disciplined, and that the children's needs are met in a timely manner. Shelter staff also reprimands parents if they are found in violation of shelter rules regarding parenting. Therefore, parents are apt to function at the standards of the shelter at least for the duration of their shelter stay. This may not be a lasting adjustment but solely for the time that they are forced to engage in "public mothering". It would be of much interest to assess these parents' parenting quality after they have moved into their private homes.

Self-concept of Homeless and Housed Children

As hypothesized, homeless children exhibited significantly lower global self-concept than housed children. In fact, about twice as many homeless (35.48%) than housed children (17.86%) scored in the lowest level of global self-concept. This finding is consistent with previous literature, which suggests that homelessness undermines children's self-confidence and perceptions of the physical, academic, and socioemotional well-being (Bassuk and Rosenberg, 1988).

Homeless girls, when compared with housed girls exhibited significantly poorer global and anxiety self-concept. No significant difference was found among the boys, which confirms previous findings that homelessness has a more negative effect on girls than boys (Rescorla et al., 1991). Rescorla et al. (1991) found that both boys and girls exhibited negative outcomes in response to homelessness, however, homeless girls, exhibited significantly more negative outcomes in response to homelessness. Homeless girls exhibited significantly more internal behavioral problems, while the boys exhibited more external behavioral problems.

Children who live in poverty are often reared by psychologically distressed parents who have minimal emotional resources left for them. Homeless children are suspected to be at greater disadvantage than housed poor children due to the added stressors of unstable housing.

Research indicates that children with better parent-child relations and children who do not evidence ambivalent attachment patterns in relation to their parents have higher self-concept (Groze, 1992). Again, the shelter experience may jeopardize parent-child relations, as shelter personnel assume parenting responsibilities and treat mothers condescendingly (Boxill and Beaty, 1987). Children lose respect for their mothers and their families, leading to lower level of self-concept. Once again, the uniqueness of the experiences of the homeless in comparison to the poor in general and the added negative impact of homelessness to the inherent oppositional consequences of poverty are brought into focus.

The literature clearly predicts that poverty and the negative experiences of the parents (McLoyd, 1990), are likely to reflect negatively on the children, resulting in negative self-concept (Markus et al., 1982). The findings of this study suggest that the experiences of both the homeless and housed populations are negative (Bassuk, 1991, 1993; Bauman, 1993; Lorion and Saltzman, 1993), therefore, the children are likely to have impaired self-concepts. However, although more of the homeless children often have low self-concept in most of the domains, the children in general reflected average global self-concept, and average and high self-concept in the specific domains.

The report of higher than expected self-concept by the children of this study is not a novel phenomenon. Developmental research points out that young children report exaggerated self-esteem despite adversities (Connell, Spence and Aber, 1994). It should be underscored, however, that although the children's report of their self-concept may be inflated, homeless children tended to perceive themselves as less competent. This supports the notion that homelessness may derail normative developmental trajectory.

BEHAVIORAL PROBLEMS OF HOMELESS AND HOUSED CHILDREN

As expected, homeless children exhibited significantly more external behavioral problems than housed children. Specifically, approximately twice as many homeless children (22.97%) than housed children (10.96%) fell in the clinical range on external behavioral problems. Thus, homeless children were more likely than their housed counterpart to exhibit problems with aggression, temper tantrums, stubbornness, attention-seeking behaviors, and destructive behaviors. These findings suggest the impaired psychological well-being of homeless children and a need for psychiatric evaluation and intervention, above that of poor housed children.

Current findings also revealed that homeless boys exhibited significantly more total behavioral problems than housed boys. These findings are consistent with those of Rescorla et al. (1991) who found that homeless boys were more likely to show acting out behaviors such as aggression, destructiveness, disobedience, and temper outbursts than housed boys. However, Rescorla et al. (1991) did not find significant differences in the external behavioral behavioral problems of homeless and housed boys.

When considering the behavioral problems of homeless children, an immediate place to look for an explanation is the stressful context in which they live. Poor parent-child relationships and compromised family environments among homeless children will result in increased behavioral problems (McLeod et al., 1994). Increased behavioral problems have been found to be associated with maternal parenting stress (Eyberg, Bogg, and

Rodriguez, 1992) and family violence (Dyson, 1990), both of which are characteristics of homeless families.

In addition to the setting in which homeless families reside, the significantly higher level of external behavioral problems may exist among the homeless children because of the continuous distraction of the parents from their children. Children depend on their parents first to give them attention and affection. If they do not receive them, the children will act in unacceptable ways in order to get attention, whether positive or negative. There is evidence that homelessness in and of itself precipitates behavioral difficulties in children (Rafferty and Shinn, 1991).

Shelters have many rules, which are highly restrictive for children. Rules such as no running in the hallways, no loud noises, no access to other families' or residents' rooms, no outdoor play without parents' direct supervision, no use of toys except when used in the play room, and no eating outside of the dining room or kitchen are only a few of the rules that children must contend with while in shelter. Therefore, even if the children's behaviors are normative, because of the many restrictions, which constrict the normal behaviors of the children, their behaviors may appear problematic.

Homeless children in shelters are also forced to exhibit aggressive and defensive behaviors in an effort to protect their possessions from older children. Additionally, the effects of crowding could have adverse effects on the children's behavior. Group living has been found to foster interpersonal conflicts among the residence (Booth, Welch, Johnson, Higgins, Richards, and Swan, 1976), and evidence of this among homeless children in shelters may be their expression of higher external behavioral problems.

A common experience among parents living in shelters is the feeling of lost autonomy (Bauman, 1993; Boxill and Beaty, 1987). The parents who have been established heads of household in their single parent families are subjected to superior figures upon arrival into shelters. A common theme among homeless children is that they dislike when shelter staff reprimands their moms. If children's parents are being reprimanded before their eyes, the parents will lose authority and quite possibly the respect of their children, resulting in "acting-out behaviors." Children who know that their parents are "under the control" of others will be negatively affected. Some, in this case the boys, will be more prone to challenge their parents and display behaviors they are aware their parents do not endorse.

The following quote from a homeless parent describes the impact of shelter living on the parent-child relationship very well:

> "Staying in a shelter was a terrible situation for all of us in many, many ways. But perhaps the worst was that I really felt that I was losing control over the well-being of my children. I blame a lot of it on the fact that I was treated like such an imbecile. I didn't need to be reminded constantly about the stupid rules and regulations in that place. They

treat all the parents like children, which means that the kids begin to show total disrespect for their moms and dads. After all, why should my kids respect their mom who is being treated like a child herself? I couldn't wait to get out of there if only to be able to have a more normal kind of relationship with my children." (Stark, 1994, p. 557).

RELATIONSHIPS BETWEEN FAMILY FUNCTIONING VARIABLES AND CHILD OUTCOME VARIABLES

The family functioning variables most likely to be significantly related to child outcome variables among the housed were predominantly personal growth and interpersonal relationships, and parental support to a lesser extent. The family functioning variable related to child outcomes among the homeless was parental control. While there is consistency regarding some of the experiences of both groups of families, the living conditions of both groups are also different and may have different effects on the children, the parents' self-worth, and the parent-child relationship.

Parental control is a key factor in the living conditions of homeless families. Control is established by shelter staff but is enforced by the parents, whether they agree with it or not. The children are often quite aware that mom has to obey the shelter rules; therefore, they understand that control is not established and maintained by the parents but by shelter authorities. Children need to know that the head of the family is "in charge". This provides a sense of safety and security within their individual families. When this is absent it is likely that affected children will exhibit adverse outcomes, such as lower self-concept.

Personal growth measures independence, achievement orientation, intellectual-cultural orientation, active recreational orientation, and moral religious emphasis. Interpersonal relationship measures cohesion, expressiveness, and conflict within the family. These two family functioning variables were significantly related to child outcomes among the housed. Specifically, mothers' higher personal growth within the families was positively related to higher anxiety, and lower intelligence, school status, popularity and global self-concept. Mothers who are motivated toward personal growth did appear to pass on their own self-confidence on to their children.

As mentioned earlier, the housed population was drawn from a very low-income area. Poor parents have been found to deteriorate in psychological functioning, and model a sense of despondency and despair which creates a gloomy climate in the homes (Kelly, Sheldon, and Fox, 1985). A milieu of this sort does not afford for achievement orientation, independence, and intellectual-cultural orientation or active-recreation orientation. The absence of these factors in the family environment has made deficient personal growth a salient descriptor of the family and predictor of child outcome.

While the homeless families may also be challenged by the consequences of poverty, that is feelings of despondency, despair and deteriorated psychological functioning, the influences of the imposed authority upon their parenting role may be more pronounced than those of poverty in general. When a mother is stripped of all her belongings; home, clothing, car, money, and even spouse, all she has left are usually her children—her parenting role. She might have lost most of what defined her sense of dignity, but the one thing she has left is her parenting role. However, upon going into shelter, her parenting role is often taken from her. Since the parent-child relationship is such a key factor in the family and appears to be most influential on the children's outcome while in shelter, an interference of it may contribute to impaired psychological well-being of children, more than other family functioning variables.

PREDICTORS OF CHILD WELL-BEING

Family processes have been found to mediate child outcome among poor children, children exposed to community violence, and other stressful situations. In this study the predictive value of family process variables in predicting child outcomes seemed stronger among the housed than the homeless population. Homelessness may indeed be a unique experience that overshadows family process factors. Homeless and housed families are similar in many ways, but the findings of this study also indicate that they are different in specific domains, and are experiencing dissimilar consequences as a result of their unique situations. In particular, child outcomes may be differentially affected due to housing status.

Parental control was predictive of more negative child outcomes such as poorer happiness and anxiety self-concept, and higher internal and total behavioral problems. More controlling parents were more likely to use rigid, coercive methods of control in their parenting practices. As discussed earlier, parenting characteristics and quality are influenced by the living conditions of families in shelter. In this study poorer parenting quality, as defined as low structure, low support, and high control, led to poorer anxiety self-concept among girls that is a perception that they have high anxiety levels.

Among the housed families, personal growth, parental support, and interpersonal relationships were related to child outcomes. Parental support was predictive of fewer internal behavioral problems and fewer total behavioral problems. Maternal personal growth within the family was associated with better anxiety self-concept. All predictors, except interpersonal relationships emerged as positive predictors of self-concept. This brings the quality of the housed families' interpersonal relationships into questioning, a family functioning variable that is readily affected by family disputes and family violence.

In contrast to the homeless children, housed children's functioning was related to intrafamilial relationships and parents' social networks. When one considers that the housed children in this study were exposed to pervasive community and family violence (a theme which emerged from open-ended questions posed to children), it is quite reasonable that the predicting variables are predominantly family processes variables. Family process variables that predicted child outcome were personal growth which predicted better anxiety self-concept; personal growth which predicted high intelligence and school status self-concept; personal growth which predicted high popularity self-concept; personal growth which predicted high global self-concept; interpersonal relationships which predicted fewer internal behavioral problems and interpersonal relationships which predicted better anxiety self-concept.

It is also quite reasonable that intrafamilial relationships negatively predict a positive child outcome such as self-concept. A life of poverty engenders a sense of hopelessness and despair. Community violence also engenders fear and hopelessness (Lorion and Saltzman, 1993), emotional deficits that are strongly related to suffocated personal growth. Children who reside in violent homes and communities report experiencing less parental protectiveness and greater vulnerability (parental support) (Lorion and Saltzman, 1993), a predictor that is highlighted for the housed families.

Stressful conditions are related to anxiety for children and adults alike (Gold, Milan, Mayhall, and Johnson, 1994; Hodges, Tierney, and Buchsbaum, 1984). Anxiety self-concept measures the children's perceptions of their anxiety level. Both groups of families reside in stressful environments and anxiety self-concept was a predicted outcome variable in both groups. The outcome variable that appeared to be most influenced by family processes, which are mostly parenting quality variables, was anxiety self-concept. This could mean that anxiety self-concept or anxiety itself is a key factor in the measure of children's psychological well-being and that the family process variable that influences it most is parenting quality.

Total parental quality (parental support, control, and structure) was one of the variables with the strongest and a negative influence on anxiety self-concept among the housed and total parental quality and parental control had the strongest and a negative influence among the homeless group. However, family functioning variables were most influential among the housed group for child outcome variables while parent-child relation was most influential among the homeless group. This difference between the two groups points back to the unique experiences of each group; the living conditions of the homeless and the intrafamilial relationships of the housed.

Another final point for consideration is, although intrafamilial relationships are well pronounced negative influences on anxiety self-concept among the housed, parental quality also emerged as a negative predictor both in the housed and homeless group. Therefore, although community factors that affect the intrafamilial relationships are fairly forcible, the parent-child relationship is equally, if not more influential.

Above all, parenting quality was most influential on child outcome. Although the negative environments of both group of families may affect family processes, the relationship between the parents and the children appear to affect child outcome most.

CONCLUSIONS

Poverty does have deleterious effects on families. Both the homeless and housed groups in this study live in poverty, therefore there are some inherent similarities between both groups. Research has shown that conditions of poverty interfere with ones motivation to achieve (Edelstein, 1972), the parent-child relationship (McLoyd, 1990), and it elicits stress (Whipple, 1992). Both populations of this study displayed similarly compromised parent-child relations.

While many families of this nation live in poverty and are all similar on that single characteristic, they differ on many others. If the two populations in this study are to be considered, it can be seen that both populations are similar, because they are both poor, but differ on other characteristics. Homelessness is a direct outcome of poverty, yet homelessness has unique consequences that poverty in general does not have. Similarly, community violence has been found to be more prevalent in urban, low socio-economic communities (Cooley-Quille, Turner, and Biedel, 1995), but its effects are also very different from that of poverty itself.

It has been argued that policies and programs to assist homeless families or prevent homelessness among families must address the problem in the larger context of poverty (Masten, 1992). Others have argued that chronic homelessness is linked to poverty; therefore the solution is the availability of adequate, affordable housing (Martin, 1991). While there is consensus that chronic homelessness is linked to poverty, there is disagreement with the positions that homelessness should be addressed from the larger context of poverty and that the only solution is adequate, affordable housing. Both groups lack financial resources, and as shown by the findings of this study both groups experienced unstable housing histories. Nevertheless, one group has resorted to shelter or motel for housing and one group has managed to maintain private housing, even if it is not optimal. The groups differ significantly on personal growth and interpersonal relationship, with the homeless families exhibiting less personal growth attributes and poorer interpersonal relationships. Some questions that research should seek to answer are: "Why does one group of families resort to shelter and one does not?"; and "What are the contributing factors to the difference in interpersonal relationship and personal growth?" The fact that these questions even exist is a clear indication that the homelessness crisis goes far beyond a lack of affordable housing.

A home should be basic to one's life. It should be the center of one's existence—a place where one can feel safe, secured, be one's self without reservation, feel accepted, and have one's needs met. The absence of this basic provision appears to lead to experiences that disrupt both the children's and the parents' lives, the children's behavior, relationships (family and parent-child), and children's feelings about themselves. The lack of a home is an experience that housed families do not have to face, it is an experience that is unique to homeless families with exclusive outcomes. It is undebatable that poverty is stressful, but the multiple and simultaneous stress of poverty and homelessness must have a stronger negative effect than poverty itself.

POLICY AND PROGRAM IMPLICATIONS

The field of social sciences has fallen prey to diverting attention from the underlying causes of homelessness to reinforcing stereotypes about homeless individuals and families. This study has attempted to do the opposite by examining the factors that differentiate homeless families from housed low-income families.

This study should be another indication to policy makers, service providers and social scientists that homelessness is not solely an economic issue. There are psychological dysfunctions that lead to homelessness and experiences that are incurred during homelessness that negatively affect its victims.

One area that is strongly affected by the experience of homelessness is the parent-child relationship. Many factors that contribute to family homelessness as well as shelter living may impair parental functioning. The large numbers of families in one place, shelter rules, and the frequent moves from one shelter to another often do not facilitate autonomy, privacy, independence or stability. While shelters are in place to assist homeless individuals and families, shelter residents' personal feelings are reported to be quite the opposite.

The findings of this study show the following: homeless children have poorer psychological well-being than poor housed children; homeless families have less personal growth attributes and poorer interpersonal relationships; and homeless families have few social networks, less social embeddedness, and less perceived support. These findings indicate that shelter programs should be designed to meet a range of needs that are broader than the need for food and shelter. Shelter programs should include therapeutic services specifically designed for the children in response to the existing behavioral problems and low self-concept. Services should also address the entire family unit to ameliorate interpersonal relationships and instill personal growth attributes in the families, particularly

Implications of Findings 91

the heads of households. Shelter administrators should also structure the shelter program in a way that will allow shelter residents to maintain ties with social networks, both formal and informal. Shelter staff, for example case managers, should encourage shelter residents to utilize the resources they have outside of the shelter rather than isolate themselves and become solely dependent upon shelter staff and other shelter residents. This would possibly allow them to see that they do have more perceived social support than they think, if that is the case.

Shelters are quite costly (an average nightly perdium, per person, in the area that this study was conducted is currently $42.00) when compared to private dwellings (an average of $750/month for a two bedroom apartment). An apartment that would provide private dwelling, is cheaper ($9,000 for one year versus $30,00 for a mother and two children), less crowded, give personal space and a sense of home. This would reduce feelings of lost autonomy, subservience, anger, helplessness, and fear. Program participants would also be more receptive of services, since they would feel less aggravated at staff who constantly supervise, reprimand them, and enforce shelter rules.

Children would continue to view the parents as head of household, and maintain respect for them rather than shelter staff. Parents would be able to share their value systems with their children, and parents would be able to engage in "private parenting", a factor of much importance to the parent-child relationship.

Shelter administrators should manage shelters with a deliberate effort to keep families autonomous, ensuring that the role of the parents is preserved. Also, shelter rules and regulations should not serve as barriers to the attempts made by the residents to pursue economic resources or to maintain social ties.

Homeless families should use shelters strictly under emergency situations for very short stays. Continued services should be delivered to families in private units, and services, policies and funding should be directed toward private housing with appropriate services (emotional, physical, educational, and social) for the entire family, not just the parents. Services should include parenting education, self-esteem building groups, family and individual counseling that address interpersonal relationships with family members and spouse, counseling/therapy for children (individual and group) and work groups (educational and therapeutic) that address the antecedents of homelessness. Financial planning and money management, life skills, and goal setting should also be an integral part of the services that these programs offer.

LIMITATIONS OF THE STUDY

(1) The assessment of the families' process resources was solely self reported. The parents' perception of their family functioning may be positively exaggerated; therefore a valid assessment may not be acquired.

(2) Although all children living in shelters were categorized as homeless, all those children may not describe themselves as homeless, the children's perception of their housing status may diffuse the true effects of homelessness on their self-concept.

(3) An examination of the differences in the homeless families who live in apartments with those who live in shelters probably would further explain the effects of the living conditions of shelter life.

(4) A larger sample size from a wider geographic area would have been more representative of the population, therefore generalizations may be limited.

(5) The use of a self report measure of the children's self-concept may not be a true reflection of their self-concept. Also, the younger children were unable to complete the instrument.

(6) There was no income verification for the participants of the study. therefore, it is not verified by means of income if one group was poorer than the other.

(7) The high stressed, high violence exposure housed group may not typify low-income families, resulting in a less than adequate comparable group for the homeless.

Recommendations for Future Research

Additional research that seeks to identify the difference in family functioning and children's psychological well-being in homeless and housed low-income families is necessary.

In order to obtain a clearer understanding of the effects of homelessness on families studies that examine the function of the length of homelessness and the living conditions/dynamics of shelter living are needed. An additional approach to a close examination of the effects of homelessness on families is to conduct longitudinal studies that look at families while in shelter and after being placed in affordable housing. The length of time in housing, and the quality of life, children's psychological well-being, and family functioning before and after being placed in shelter are variables that should be examined. Research should also examine the role of anxiety self-concept and anxiety itself in the definition of children's psychological well-being and the role that parent-child relationship plays in affecting it.

Finally, community violence and its effects on young children and their families must be examined. Both populations under discussion live in poverty, and research has shown that community violence is at higher rates in low-income communities. Homelessness and poverty are clearly inseparable, and community violence and poverty may be affecting child outcome in the same way. Further research will help to clarify this.

Appendix A

RESEARCH SUMMARY/DESCRIPTION

Title of Research
Children's psychological well-being as a function of housing status and process resources in low-income families

Purpose of the study:
To explore the effects of homelessness on the parent-child relationships and its effects on the children's self-concept. The parent-child relationships will be assessed by measuring the families' emotional (process) resources. The study will include two groups of families — currently homeless and housed low-income families. The housed group is included in the study because these families will allow the researcher to explore potential differences in the parent-child relationships and the children's self-concept for both groups of families.

Instruments:
The Family Environment Scale (FES), The Parenting Dimensions Inventory (PDI), The Family Support Scale (FSS), Social Embeddedness Questionnaire (SEQ), and the Child Behavior Checklist (CBCL). The parents will respond to these questionnaires.

The children will respond to the Piers-Harris Children's Self-concept Scale.

Participants:
Homeless and low-income housed families with children between the ages of four and eight. Homeless families will be residing in shelters. The children who are participating in the study will be residing with their parents.

Method:
This researcher will administer the instruments in small groups to parents and on an individual basis to the children. Confidentiality will be maintained for all participants. The names of the participants will not be used on any document, and the names of the site of the research will not be entered on any written document.

Parent interviews will take approximately 1 hour and children interviews will take approximately 30 minutes.

APPENDIX B

PARENTS EARN A QUICK $10

Do you have a child living with you who is between four and eight years of age?

We will interview your children about their friends and how they feel about themselves for about 30 minutes.

We will interview you for about one hour.

We will ask you and your children questions about how the family members relate to one another, how the children feel about themselves, and how they get along with other children.

If you want to be interviewed please inform shelter staff or your DSS case worker.

APPENDIX C

CONSENT FORM

I _____ agree to participate in the research to be conducted by the University of Maryland at College Park. My child or children _____ will also participate.

- I understand that questions will be asked about how my family members interact with one other, how my child feel about him/herself, and how he/she gets along with other children.

- I understand that neither my name nor my child's name will be placed on any document used in the study.

- I understand that if I wish to end the interview for myself or my child at any time I can do so.

- If I am participating in a homeless services program (a shelter or a motel for homeless families), I understand that the administrators of these programs are not liable for my participation in the study.

_____   _____
Parent Signature   Date

APPENDIX D

STANDARDIZED INSTRUCTIONS—BEFORE PARENT INTERVIEWS

Hi, my name is Rosemarie. Thank you very much for agreeing to be interviewed. I will be asking you some questions about your family and how all of you interact with one another. I will also be asking you some questions about how you relate to your child who is also being interviewed.

I would much prefer if you complete the interview, however if you choose to end the interview for you and your child at anytime you are free to do so. Everything we talk about will be held confidential. Your name will not be placed on any document that are used in the study, instead you will be assigned a code number.

Thanks again for agreeing to participate.

Do you have any questions?

(Give time for response)

OK, we'll begin.

APPENDIX E

STANDARDIZED INSTRUCTIONS—BEFORE CHILD INTERVIEWS

Hi, my name is _____. I will be asking you some questions about yourself, your family, and your friends. Also I will be showing you some pictures of things that you and your friends use and play with a lot.

If you get tired you can let me know and we can take a break, or if you feel like stopping just let me know and we will stop. I will not tell anyone anything you tell me unless you are in danger and I need to protect you.

Do you want to ask anything?

(Give time for response)

OK, we'll begin.

APPENDIX F
PARTICIPANT SCREENING SHEET
(HOMELESS)

ID #: _____

Race: ___ African American: ___ Caucasian: ___ Latino: ___
Other: ___
Age: _____ Grade Completed: < High School: ____
High School/GED: ____
                          Some college: ____ College graduate: ____
Length of homeless: Exact length: _____ OR
___ < 3 months   ___ 4-8 months   ___ 9-12 months
___ > 12 months

1. Over the past three months where have you lived?
   _____
   _____
   _____

2. Have you lived in doubled up housing situation(s) in the past year?
   ___ YES   ___ NO

3. If yes, was it your housing?   ___ YES   ___ NO

4. Do you have a child/ren between the ages of 4 and 8 living with you now?   ___ YES   ___ NO

5. Are you currently employed?   ___ YES   ___ NO
   Full-time: _____   Part-time: _____

TARGET CHILD
1. Age: _____   2. Date of birth: _____
3. Gender: ___ Male ___ Female
4. Birth Order: ___ First Born   ___ Middle   ___ Last
5. Currently attending school?   ___ YES   ___ NO
6. Repeated any grades?   ___ YES   ___ NO
7. Grade in school: _____

APPENDIX G

PARTICIPANT SCREENING SHEET
(HOUSED)

ID #: _____

Have you ever been homeless? ___ YES ___ NO

Race: African American: ___ Caucasian: ___ Latino: ___
Other: ___
Age: ___ Grade Completed: < High School: ___
High School/GED: ___
　　　　　　　　　Some college: ___ College graduate: ___

1. Do you have a child/ren between the ages of 4 and 8 living with you now? ___ YES ___ NO
2. Have you shared housing with someone in the past year?
   ___ YES ___ NO
3. If yes, was it your housing?
   ___ YES ___ NO
4. Have you lived in doubled up housing situation(s) in the past year?
   ___ YES ___ NO
4. Are you currently employed? ___ YES ___ NO
   Full-time: ___ YES ___ NO

TARGET CHILD
1. Age: _____ 2. Date of birth: _____
3. Gender: ___ Male ___ Female
4. Birth Order: ___ First Born ___ Middle ___ Last
5. Currently attending school? ___ YES ___ NO
6. Repeated any grades? ___ YES ___ NO
7. Grade in school: _____

ID #: _____
Housing Status: _____

APPENDIX H

FAMILY SUPPORT SCALE
(ENACTED SUPPORT)

I'd like to talk with you about some of the people who may have helped you in raising your child. I'd like to ask you how helpful some specific people are, like your parents or members of your church, in raising your family.

The alternatives are:
- 4 - Extremely helpful,
- 3 - Very helpful,
- 2 - Generally helpful,
- 1 - Sometimes helpful,
- 0 - Not at all helpful, and
- "." - Not applicable (doesn't apply).

Please think about the last 3 to 6 months. As I read the name of each person or group, I'd like you to tell me how helpful they've been to your family in the last 3 to 6 months.

In the last 3 to 6 months, how helpful was each in raising your child...

_____ 1. Your parents
_____ 2. Your relatives/kin
_____ 3. Your friends
_____ 4. Your partner, husband, wife
_____ 5. Your partner's parents
_____ 6. Your partner's relatives/kin
_____ 7. Your partner's friends
_____ 8. Your own children
_____ 9. Other parents
_____ 10. Co-workers
_____ 11. Parent groups
_____ 12. Social groups/clubs
_____ 13. Church
_____ 14. Your family or child's doctor(s)
_____ 15. Professional helpers like social workers, therapists, teachers, etc.
_____ 16. Professional agencies like social services or mental health agencies
_____ 17. Your child's Head Start program
_____ 18. Other school/day care center

ID #: _____
Housing Status: _____

APPENDIX I

SOCIAL EMBEDDEDNESS QUESTIONNAIRE
(SOCIAL EMBEDDEDNESS)

I'd like to ask you some questions about the number of people you can count on for help or support. These are people who can physically help you with your child/en or people who you can talk to when you need to.

As I ask the questions please give me a number between 0 and 10 or more.

0___1___2___3___4___5___6___7___8___9___10
                                                                         or more

The questions are:

<u>Numeric Response</u>

_____ (1) How many people can you truly count on for help in times of need?

_____ (2) How many friends/relatives do you see or talk to once a week or more?

_____ (3) How many people would be able to take care of your children for several hours if needed?

_____ (4) How many adults, other than your partner, do you have regular talks with?

TOTAL SCORE _____

| ID #: |
| Housing Status: |

APPENDIX J
THE FAMILY ENVIRONMENT SCALE

I will be reading you some statements about your family. You are to decide which of these statements are true of your family and which are false. If you think the statement is *True or mostly True* of your family, say "*True*". If you think the statement is *False or Mostly False* of your family, say "*False*".

You may feel that some of the statements are true for some family members and false for others. Say *True* if the statement is *True* for most members. Say *False* if the statement is *False* for most members. If the members are evenly divided, decide what is the stronger overall impression and answer accordingly.

1. Family members really help and support one another. — True — False

2. Family members often keep feelings to themselves. — True — False

3. We fight a lot in our family. — True — False

4. We don't do things on our own very often in our family. — True — False

5. We feel it is important to be the best at whatever we do. — True — False

6. We often talk about political and social problems. — True — False

7. We spend most weekends and evenings at home. — True — False

8. Family members attend church, synagogue, or Sunday School fairly often. — True — False

9. Activities in our family are pretty carefully planned. — True — False

| FES, Page 2 |

10.	Family members are rarely ordered around.	True	False
11.	We often seem to be killing time at home.	True	False
12.	We say anything we want around home.	True	False
13.	Family members rarely become openly angry.	True	False
14.	In our family, we are strongly encouraged to be independent.	True	False
15.	Getting ahead in life is very important in our family.	True	False
16.	We rarely go to lectures, plays, and concerts.	True	False
17.	Friends often come over for dinner or to visit.	True	False
18.	We don't say prayers in our family.	True	False
19.	We are generally very neat and orderly.	True	False
20.	There are very few rules to follow in our family.	True	False
21.	We put a lot of energy into what we do at home.	True	False
22.	It's hard to "blow off steam" at home without upsetting someone.	True	False
23.	Family members sometimes get so angry they sometimes throw things.	True	False
24.	We thinks things out for ourselves in our family	True	False
25.	How much money a person makes is not very important.	True	False

Appendix J

| FES, Page 3 |

26.	Learning about new and different things is very important in our family.	True	False
27.	Nobody in our family is active in sports, Little League, bowling, etc.	True	False
28.	We often talk about the religious meaning of Christmas, Passover, or other holidays.	True	False
29.	It's often hard to find things when you need them in our household.	True	False
30.	There is one family member who makes most of the decisions.	True	False
31.	There is a feeling of togetherness in our family.	True	False
32.	We tell each other about our personal problems	True	False
33.	Family members hardly ever lose their tempers.	True	False
34.	We come and go as we want in our family.	True	False
35.	We believe in competition and "may the best man wins."	True	False
36.	We are not that interested in cultural activities.	True	False
37.	We often go to movies, sports events, camping, etc.	True	False
38.	We don't believe in heaven or hell.	True	False
39.	Being on time is very important in our family.	True	False
40.	There are set ways of doing things at home.	True	False

FES, Page 4

41.	We rarely volunteer when something has to be done at home.	True	False
42.	If we feel like doing something on the spur of the moment we often just pick up and go.	True	False
43.	Family members often criticize each other.	True	False
44.	There is very little privacy in our family.	True	False
45.	We always strive to do things just a little better the next time.	True	False
46.	We rarely have intellectual discussions.	True	False
47.	Everyone in our family has a hobby or two.	True	False
48.	Family members have strict ideas about what is right and wrong.	True	False
49.	People change their minds often in our family.	True	False
50.	There is a strong emphasis on following rules in our family.	True	False
51.	Family members really back each other up.	True	False
52.	Someone usually gets upset if you complain in our family.	True	False
53.	Family members sometimes hit each other.	True	False
54.	Family members almost always rely on themselves when a problem comes up.	True	False
55.	Family members rarely worry about job promotions, school, grades, etc.	True	False
56.	Someone in our family plays a musical instrument.	True	False

FES, Page 5

57.	Family members are not very involved in recreational activities outside work or school.	True	False
58.	We believe there are some things you just have to take on faith.	True	False
59.	Family members make sure their rooms are neat.	True	False
60.	Everyone has an equal say in family decisions.	True	False
61.	There is very little group spirit in our family.	True	False
62.	Money and paying bill is openly talked about in our family.	True	False
63.	If there's disagreement in our family, we try hard to smooth things over and keep the peace.	True	False
64.	Family members strongly encourage each others to stand up for their rights.	True	False
65.	In our family, we don't try that hard to succeed.	True	False
66.	Family members often go to the library.	True	False
67.	Family members sometimes attend courses or take lessons for some hobby or interest (outside of school).	True	False
68.	In our family each person has different ideas about what is right and wrong.	True	False
69.	Each person's duties are clearly identified in our family.	True	False
70.	We can do whatever we want in our family.	True	False
71.	We really get along with each other.	True	False

[FES, Page 6]

72.	We are usually careful about what we say to each other.	True	False
73.	Family members often try to one-up or out-do each other.	True	False
74.	Its hard to be by yourself without hurting someone's feelings in our household.	True	False
75.	"Work before play" is the rule in our family.	True	False
76.	Watching TV is more important than reading in our family.	True	False
77.	Family members go out a lot.	True	False
78.	The Bible is a very important book in our family.	True	False
79.	Money is not handled very carefully in our family.	True	False
80.	Rules are pretty inflexible in our household.	True	False
81.	There is plenty of time and attention for every one in our family.	True	False
82.	There are a lot of spontaneous discussions in our family.	True	False
83.	In our family we believe we don't ever get anywhere by raising your voice.	True	False
84.	We are not really encouraged to speak up for ourselves in our family.	True	False
85.	Family members are often compared with others as to how well they are doing at work or school.	True	False
86.	Family members really like music, art and literature.	True	False

FES, Page 7

87. Our main form of entertainment is watching TV or listening to the radio. — True — False

88. Family members believe that if you sin you will be punished. — True — False

89. Dishes are usually done immediately after eating. — True — False

90. You can't get away with much in our family. — True — False

ID #: _____
Housing Status: _____

APPENDIX K
PARENTING DIMENSIONS INVENTORY (PDI)

For the following questions, you will be asked about your attitudes and behavior toward the child who is also being interviewed in this study.

You can respond to the questions with a number between 1 and 6. This response card (<u>Point to respond card #1</u>) tells you what the numbers mean. Give the number which most closely applies to you and your child who is also being interviewed.

1 - Not at all like me
2 - Slightly like me
3 - Somewhat like me
4 - Fairly like me
5 - Quite like me
6 - Highly like me

_____ 1. I encourage my child to talk about his or her troubles.

_____ 2. I always follow through on discipline for my child, no matter how long it takes.

_____ 3. Sometimes it is so long between the time my child misbehaves and the chance for me to deal with it that I just let it go.

_____ 4. I do not allow my child to get angry with me.

_____ 5. There are times I just don't have the energy to make my child behave as he/she should.

_____ 6. My child can often talk me into letting him/her off easier than I had intended.

_____ 7. My child convinces me to change my mind after I have refused request.

_____ 8. I think a child should be encouraged to do things better than other children.

_____ 9. My child and I have warm, close moments together.

| PDI, Page 2 |

_____ 10. I encourage my child to be curious, to explore, and to question things.

_____ 11. I find it interesting and educational to be with my child for long periods.

_____ 12. I don't think children should be given sexual information.

_____ 13. I believe a child should be seen and not heard.

_____ 14. I believe it is not always a good idea to encourage children to talk about their worries because it can upset them even more.

_____ 15. I encourage my child to express his/her opinions.

_____ 16. I make sure my child knows that I appreciate what he/she tries to accomplish.

_____ 17. I let my child know how ashamed and disappointed I am when he/she misbehaves.

_____ 18. I believe in toilet training a child as soon as possible.

_____ 19. I believe that most children change their minds so often that it is hard to take their opinions seriously.

_____ 20. I have little or no difficulties sticking to my rules for my child even when close relatives (including when grandparents) are there.

_____ 21. When I let my child talk about his/her troubles, he/she ends up complaining even more.

_____ 22. I expect my child to be grateful to his/her parents, and appreciate all the advantages he/she has.

_____ 23. Once I decide how to deal with a misbehavior of my child, I follow through on it.

_____ 24. I respect my child's opinions and encourage him/her to express them.

Appendix K

PDI, Page 3

_____ 25. I never threaten my child with a punishment unless I am sure I will carry it out.

_____ 26. I believe that once a family rule has been made, it should be strictly enforced without exception.

APPENDIX L
CHILD BEHAVIOR CHECKLIST (CBCL)

0=NOT TRUE (AS FAR AS YOU KNOW)
1=SOMEWHAT OR SOMETIMES TRUE   2=VERY TRUE OR OFTEN TRUE

1. Acts too young for his/her age   0 1 2
2. Allergy (describe): _____
   _____   0 1 2
3. Argues a lot   0 1 2
4. Asthma   0 1 2
5. Behaves like opposite sex   0 1 2
6. Bowel movement outside toilet   0 1 2
7. Bragging, boasting   0 1 2
8. Can't concentrate, can't pay attention for long   0 1 2
9. Can't get his/her mind off certain thoughts: obsessions
   (describe): _____
   _____   0 1 2
10. Can't sit still, restless, or hyperactive   0 1 2
11. Clings to adults or too dependent   0 1 2
12. Complains of loneliness   0 1 2
13. Confused or seems to be in a fog   0 1 2
14. Cries a lot   0 1 2
15. Cruel to animals   0 1 2
16. Cruelty, bullying, or meanness to others   0 1 2
17. Daydreams or gets lost in his/her thoughts   0 1 2
18. Deliberately harms self or attempts suicide   0 1 2
19. Demands a lot of attention   0 1 2
20. Destroys his/her own things   0 1 2
21. Destroys things belonging to his/her family or
    other friends   0 1 2
22. Disobedient at home   0 1 2
23. Disobedient at school   0 1 2
24. Doesn't eat well   0 1 2
25. Doesn't get along with other children   0 1 2
26. Doesn't seem to feel guilty after misbehaving   0 1 2
27. Easily jealous   0 1 2
28. Eats or drinks things that are not food-doesn't include
    sweets (describe): _____   0 1 2
29. Fears certain animals: situations or places other than
    school (describe):_____
    _____   0 1 2
30. Fears going to school   0 1 2

0=NOT TRUE (AS FAR AS YOU KNOW)
1=SOMEWHAT OR SOMETIMES TRUE   2=VERY TRUE OR OFTEN TRUE

31. Fears he/she might think or do something bad	0	1	2
32. Feels he/she has to be perfect	0	1	2
33. Feels or complains that no one love him/her	0	1	2
34. Feels others are out to get him/her	0	1	2
35. Feels worthless or inferior	0	1	2
36. Gets hurt a lot, accident-prone	0	1	2
37. Gets in many fights	0	1	2
38. Gets teased a lot	0	1	2
39. Hangs around with children who get in trouble	0	1	2
40. Hears sounds or voices that aren't there (describe): _____	0	1	2
41. Impulsive or acts without thinking	0	1	2
42. Likes to be alone	0	1	2
43. Lying or cheating	0	1	2
44. Bites fingernails	0	1	2
45. Nervous, high-strung, or tense	0	1	2
46. Nervous movements or twitching (describe): _____ _____	0	1	2
47. Nightmares	0	1	2
48. Not liked by other children	0	1	2
49. Constipated, doesn't move bowels	0	1	2
50. Too fearful or anxious	0	1	2
51. Feels dizzy	0	1	2
52. Feels too guilty	0	1	2
53. Overeating	0	1	2
54. Overtired	0	1	2
55. Overweight	0	1	2
56. Physical problems without known medical cause			
a. Aches and pains	0	1	2
b. Headaches	0	1	2
c. Nausea, feels sick	0	1	2
d. Problems with eyes (describe):_____ _____	0	1	2
e. Rashes or other skin problems	0	1	2
f. Stomach aches or cramps	0	1	2
g. Vomiting, throwing up	0	1	2
h. Other (describe): _____ _____	0	1	2

Appendix L

0=NOT TRUE (AS FAR AS YOU KNOW)
1=SOMEWHAT OR SOMETIMES TRUE   2=VERY TRUE OR OFTEN TRUE

57. Physically attacks people	0	1	2
58. Picks nose, skin, or other parts of body (describe): _____	0	1	2
59. Plays with own sex parts in public	0	1	2
60. Plays with own sex parts too much	0	1	2
61. Poor school work	0	1	2
62. Poorly coordinated or clumsy	0	1	2
63. Prefers playing with older children	0	1	2
64. Prefers playing with younger children	0	1	2
65. Refuses to talk	0	1	2
66. Repeats certain acts over and over: compulsions (describe): _____	0	1	2
67. Runs away from home	0	1	2
68. Screams a lot	0	1	2
69. Secretive, keeps things to self	0	1	2
70. Sees things that aren't there (describe): _____ _____	0	1	2
71. Self-conscious or easily embarrassed	0	1	2
72. Sets fires	0	1	2
73. Sexual problems (describe): _____ _____	0	1	2
74. Showing off or clowning	0	1	2
75. Shy or timid	0	1	2
76. Sleeps more than most children	0	1	2
77. Sleeps more than most children during the day and/or night (describe): _____	0	1	2
78. Smears or plays with bowel movement	0	1	2
79. Speech problem (describe): _____ _____	0	1	2
80. Stares blankly	0	1	2
81. Steals at home	0	1	2
82. Steals outside of home	0	1	2
83. Stores up things he/she doesn't need (describe): ____ _____	0	1	2

0=NOT TRUE (AS FAR AS YOU KNOW)

0=NOT TRUE (AS FAR AS YOU KNOW)
1=SOMEWHAT OR SOMETIMES TRUE   2=VERY TRUE OR OFTEN TRUE

84. Strange behavior (describe): _____ _____	0	1	2
85. Strange ideas (describe): _____ _____	0	1	2
86. Stubborn, sullen, or irritable	0	1	2
87 Sudden changes in mood or feelings	0	1	2
88. Sulks a lot	0	1	2
89. Suspicious	0	1	2
90. Swearing or obscene language	0	1	2
91. Talks about killing self	0	1	2
92. Talks or walks in sleep (describe): _____ _____	0	1	2
93. Talks too much	0	1	2
94. Teases a lot	0	1	2
95. Temper tantrums or hot temper	0	1	2
96. Thinks about sex too much	0	1	2
97. Threatens people	0	1	2
98. Thumb-sucking	0	1	2
99. Too concerned with neatness or cleanliness	0	1	2
100. Trouble sleeping (describe): _____ _____	0	1	2
101. Truancy, skips school	0	1	2
102. Underactive, slow moving or low energy	0	1	2
103. Unhappy, sad or depressed	0	1	2
104. Unusually loud	0	1	2
105. Uses alcohol or drugs for nonmedical purposes (describe): _____	0	1	2
106. Vandalism	0	1	2
107. Wets self during the day	0	1	2
108. Wets the bed	0	1	2
109. Whining	0	1	2
110. Wishes to be of opposite sex	0	1	2
111. Withdrawn, doesn't get involved with others	0	1	2
112. Worrying	0	1	2

113. Please write in any problems your child has had that were not listed above

_____

_____

APPENDIX M

THE WAY I FEEL ABOUT MYSELF

The Piers-Harris Children's Self-concept Scale
Ellen V. Piers, Ph.D. and Dale B. Harris, Ph.D.

Published by

wps WESTERN PSYCHOLOGICAL SERVICES
Publishers and Distributors
12031 Wilshire Boulevard
Los Angeles, California 90025

Name: _____ Today's Date: _____

Age: _____ Sex (circle one): Girl   Boy   Grade: _____

School: _____ Teacher's Name (optional): _____

> **Directions**: Here is a set of statements that tell how some people feel about themselves. Read each statement and decide whether or not it describes the way you feel about yourself. If it is true or mostly true for you, circle the word "yes" next to the statement. If it is false or mostly false for you, circle the word "no". Answer every question, even if some are hard to decide. Do not circle both "yes" and "no" for the same statement.
>
> Remember that there are no right or wrong answers. Only you can tell us how you feel about yourself, so we hope you will mark the way you really feel inside.

Total Score: Raw Score _____ Percentile _____ Stanine _____

Clusters: I _____ II _____ III _____ IV _____ V _____ VI _____

1. My classmates make fun of me ....yes no
2. I am a happy person .....yes no
3. It is hard for me to make friends ....yes no
4. I am often sad ....yes no
5. I am smart ....yes no
6. I am shy ....yes no
7. I get nervous when the teacher calls on me ......yes no
8. My looks bother me .....yes no
9. When I grow up I will be an important person ....yes no
10. I get worried when we have tests in school ....yes no
11. I am unpopular ....yes no
12. I am well behaved in schoo ....yes no
13. It is usually my fault when something goes wrong ....yes no
14. I cause trouble to my family ....yes no
15. I am strong ....yes no
16. I have good ideas ....yes no
17. I am an important member of my family ....yes no
18. I usually want my own way ....yes no
19. I am good at making things with my hands ....yes no
20. I give up easily ....yes no
21. I am good in my school work ....yes no
22. I do many bad things ....yes no
23. I can draw well ....yes no
24. I am good in music ......yes no
25. I behave badly at home ...yes no
26. I am slow in finishing my school work ....yes no
27. I am an important member of my class ....yes no
28. I am nervous ....yes no
29. I have pretty eyes ....yes no
30. I can give a good report in front of the class ......yes no
31. In school I am a dreamer ..yes no
32. I pick on my bother(s) and sister(s) ....yes no
33. My friends like my ideas ..yes no
34. I often get into trouble ...yes no
35. I am obedient at home ....yes no
36. I am lucky ....yes no
37. I worry a lot ....yes no
38. My parents expect too much of me ....yes no
39. I like being the way I am ....yes no
40. I feel left out of things ....yes no
41. I have nice hair ....yes no
42. I often volunteer in school ....yes no
43. I wish I were different ....yes no
44. I sleep well at night ......yes no
45. I hate school ....yes no
46. I am among the last to be chosen for games ....yes no
47. I am sick a lot ....yes no
48. I am often mean to other people ....yes no
49. My classmates in school think I have good ideas ....yes no
50. I am unhappy ....yes no
51. I have many friends ......yes no
52. I am cheerful ....yes no
53. I am dumb about most things ....yes no
54. I am good-looking ....yes no
55. I have lots of pep ....yes no
56. I get into a lot of fights ...yes no
57. I am popular with boys ...yes no
58. People pick on me ....yes no

59. My family is disappointed in me ....yes   no
60. I have a pleasant face ....yes   no
61. When I try to make something, everything seems to go wrong ......yes   no
62. I am picked on at home ....yes   no
63. I am a leader in games and sports ....yes   no
64. I am clumsy ....yes   no
65. In games and sports, I watch instead of play ....yes   no
66. I forget what I learn ....yes   no
67. I am easy to get along with ....yes   no
68. I loose my temper easily ....yes   no
69. I am popular with girls ....yes   no
70. I am a good reader ....yes   no
71. I would rather work alone than with a group ....yes   no
72. I like my brother (sister) ....yes   no
73. I have a good figure ....yes   no
74. I am often afraid ....yes   no
75. I am always dropping or breaking things ....yes   no
76. I can be trusted ....yes   no
77. I am different from other people ....yes   no
78. I think bad thoughts ....yes   no
79. I cry easily ....yes   no
80. I am a good person ....yes   no

Code #: _____
Housing Status: _____

APPENDIX N
QUALITATIVE DATA — PARENTS

1. If there was one wish in life you could make come true, what would it be?
   _____
   _____
   _____

2. What is the most difficult part of raising your child?
   _____
   _____
   _____
   _____

3. What is the best part of raising your child?
   _____
   _____
   _____
   _____

4. A year or two from now, where do you see yourself (regarding relationships, housing, work, parenting, education etc.)?
   _____
   _____
   _____
   _____

5. The five most important things to you are :
   (i) _____
   (ii) _____
   (iii) _____
   (iv) _____
   (v) _____

ADDITIONAL INFORMATION:
_____
_____
_____
_____

Code #: _____
Housing Status: _____

APPENDIX O

QUALITATIVE DATA — CHILDREN

1. If there was one wish in life you could make come true, what would it be?
   _____
   _____

2. What do you like most about yourself and your family?
   YOURSELF: _____
   _____

   FAMILY: _____
   _____
   _____

3. Is there anything you don't like about yourself and your family?
   YOURSELF: _____
   _____

   FAMILY: _____
   _____
   _____

4. What do you like and dislike most about where you live?
   LIKE: _____
   _____

   DISLIKE: _____
   _____
   _____

Bibliography

Abidin, R. R. (1983). *Parenting stress-index manual.* Charlottsville, VA: Pediatric Psychology Press.

Achenbach, T. M. (1991). *Manual for the Child Behavior Checklist/4-18 and 1991 profile.* Burlington, VT: University of Vermont Department of Psychiatry.

Achenbach, T. M. and Edelbrock, C. (1983). *Manual for the Child Behavior Checklist and revised child behavior profile.* Burlington, VT: Queen City Printers.

Alperstein, G., and Arnstein, E. (1988). Homeless children-a challenge for pediatricians. *Pediatric Clinics of North America, 35,* 1413-1425.

Alperstein, G., Rappaport, C., and Flanigan, J. M. (1988). Health problems of homeless children in New York City. *American Journal of Public Health, 78,* 1232-1233.

Altman, H., and Firnesz, K. (1973). A role playing approach to influencing behavioral change and self-esteem. *Elementary School Guidance and Counseling, 7,* 276-281.

Amato, P. R. (1986). Marital conflict, the parent-child relationship, and self-esteem. *Family Relations, 35,* 403-410.

Anderson, S. C., Boe, T., and Smith, S. (1988). Homeless women. *Affilia, 3*(2), 62-70.

Bahr, H., and Caplow, T. (1974). *Old men drunk and sober.* New York: New York University Press.

Barrera, M. (1986). Distinctions between social support concepts, measures, and models. *American Journal of Community Psychology, 14*(4), 413-445.

Baruch, G. K. (1976). Girls who perceive themselves as competent: Some antecedents and correlates. *Psychology of Women Quarterly, 1*(1), 38-49.

Bassuk, E. (1984). The homeless problem. *Scientific America, 251,* 40-45.

Bassuk, E. (1987). The feminization of homelessness: Families in Boston shelters. *American Journal of Social Psychiatry, 7*(1), 19-23.

Bassuk, E. L. (1991). Homeless families. *Scientific American,* 66-74.

Bassuk, E. L. (1993). Social and economic hardships of homeless and other poor women. *American Journal of Orthopsychiatry, 63*(3), 340-347.

Bassuk, E. L., and Gallagher, E. M. (1990). The impact of homelessness on children. In N. A. Boxill *Homeless children. The watchers and waiters.* Chapter 3. The Haworth Press. New York.

Bassuk, E. L., and Rosenberg, L. (1990). Psychosocial characteristics of homeless children and children with homes. *Pediatrics, 85,* 257-261.

Bassuk, E. L., and Rosenberg, L. (1988). Why does family homelessness occur? A case control study. *American Journal of Public Health, 78*(7), 783-788.

Bassuk, E. L., and Rubin, L. (1987). Homeless children: A neglected population. *American Journal of Orthopsychiatry, 57*(2), 279-286.

Bassuk, E. L., Rubin, L., and Lauriat, A. S. (1986). Characteristics of sheltered homeless families. *American Journal of Public Health, 76,* 1097-1101.

Bauman, S. L. (1993). The meaning of being homeless. *Scholarly Inquiry for Nursing Practice, 7*(1), 59-70.

Baumrind, D. (1965). Parental control and parental love. *Children, 12,* 230-234.

Beckman, P. J. (1983). The influences of selected child characteristics on stress in families of handicapped infants. *American Journal of Mental Deficiency, 88,* 150-156.

Beer, J. (1989). Relationship of divorce to self-concept, self-esteem, and grade point average of fifth and sixth grade school children. *Psychological Reports, 65*(3), 1379-1383.

Belle, D. E. (1981). *The social network as a source of both stress and support to low-income mothers.* Paper presented at the biennial meeting of the Society for Research in Child Development, Boston, MA.

Belle, D. E. (1982). Social ties and social support. In D. Belle (Ed.), *Lives in Stress: Women and Depression.* Beverly Hills, CA: Sage.

Belsky, J. (1984). The determinants of parenting: A process model. *Child Development, 55,* 83-96.

Bendel, R. D., Stone, W., Field, T., and Goldstein, S. (1986). Children's effects on parenting stress in low-income, minority population. *Topics in Early Childhood Special Education, 8,* 58-71.

Bernstein, A. B., Alperstein G., and Fierman, A. H. (1988). *Health Care of Homeless Children*. Paper presented at the meeting of the American Public Health Association, Chicago.

Bishop, S., and Ingersoll, G. (1989). Effects of marital conflict and family structure on the self-concepts of pre and early adolescents. *Journal of Youth and Adolescence, 18*, 25-28.

Blasi, G. L. (1990). Social policy and social science research on homelessness. *Journal of Social Issues, 46*(4), 207-219.

Blumberg, L., Shipley, T., and Shandler, I. (1973). Skidrow and its alternatives. Philadelphia, PA: Temple University Press.

Bogue, D. (1963). *Skid Row in American Cities*. Chicago: University of Chicago.

Booth, A., Welch, S., Johnson, D. R., Higgins, P. C., Richards, P. J, and Swan, J. H. (1976). Crowding and urban crime rates. *Urban Affairs Quarterly, 11*(3), 391-308.

Bourgois, P. (1991). Everyday life in two high-risk neighborhoods. *The American Enterprise Institute, 2*(3), 63-70.

Boxill, N., and Beaty, A. (1987). Mother/child interaction among homeless women and their children in a public night shelter in Atlanta, Georgia. *Child and Youth Services, 14*(1), 49-64.

Bronfenbrenner, U. (1986). Ecology of the family as a context for human development research perspectives. *Developmental Psychology, 22*(6), 723-742.

Bruner, J. S. (1975). Poverty and childhood. *Oxford Review of Education, 1*(1), 31-50.

Calsyn, R., Quicke, J., and Harris, S. (1980). Do improved communication skills lead to increased self-esteem? *Elementary School Guidance and Counseling, 14*, 48-55.

Chan, Y. C. (1994). The parenting stress and social support of mothers who physically abuse their children in Hong Kong. *Child Abuse and Neglect, 18*(3), 261-269.

Chaukin, W., Kristal, A., and Seabornic, G. P. (1987). The reproductive experience of women living in hotels for the homeless in New York City. NY State. *Journal of Medicine, 87*, 10-13.

Churchville, V. (1987). NE tenants hope to outlast seige of drug violence. *The Washington Post*, pp. A1, A16.

Cohen, J. (1977). *Statistical power analysis for the behavioral sciences*. New York: Academic Press.

Conger, R. D., McCarty, J. A., Yang, R. K., Lahey, B. B., and Kropp, J. P. (1984). Perception of child, child-rearing values, and emotional distress as mediating links between environmental stressors and observed maternal behavior. *Child Development, 55*, 2234-2247.

Connell, J. P., Spencer, M. B., and Aber, J. L. (1994). Educational risks and resilience in African American youths: Context, self, action, and outcomes in school. *Child Development, 65*(2), 493-506.

Cooley, C. H. (1902). *Human nature and the social order.* New York: Scribner.

Cooley-Quille, M. R., Turner, S. M., and Biedel, D. C. (1995). Emotional impact of children's exposure to community violence: A preliminary study. *Journal of American Academy of Child Adolescent Psychiatry, 34*(1), 1362-1368.

Cooper, J. E., Holman, J., and Braithwaite, V. A. (1983). Self-esteem and family cohesion: The child's perspective and adjustment. *Journal of Marriage and the Family, 45*, 153-159.

Coopersmith, S. (1967). The antecedents of self-esteem. San Francisco: W. H. Freeman and Company.

Corse, S. J., Schmid, K., and Trickett, P. K. (1990). Social network characteristics of mothers in abusing and nonabusing families and their relationships to parenting beliefs. *Journal of Community Psychology, 18*, 44-59.

Creasey, G. L., and Jarvis, P. A. (1994). Relationships between parenting stress and developmental functioning among two year olds. *Infant Behavior and Development, 17*(4), 423-429.

Crnic, K. A., Greenberg, M. T., Ragozin, A. S., Robinson, M. M., and Basham, R. B. (1983). Effects of stress and social support on mothers and premature and full-term infants. *Child Development, 54*, 209-217.

Crnic, K. A., and Greenberg, M. T. (1987). Transactional relationships between perceived family style, risk status, and mother-child interactions in two year olds. *Journal of Pediatric Psychology, 12*, 343-362.

Crnic, K. A., and Greenberg, M. T. (1990). Minor parenting stress with young children. *Child Development, 61*, 1628-1637.

Crystal, S. (1984). Homeless men and homeless women: The gender gap. *Urban and Social Change, 17*(2), 2-6.

Culp, R. E., Culp, A. M., Soulis, J., and Lette, D. (1989). Self-esteem and depression in abusive, neglecting, and nonmaltreating mothers. *Infant Mental Health Journal, 10*(4), 243-251.

Dadds, M. R., Braddock, D., Cuers, S., and Elliot, A. (1993). Personal and family distress in homeless adolescents. *Community Mental Health Journal, 26*(5), 413-422.

Dager, E. Z., and Thompson, G. B. (1986). Family structure and family climate effects on black and white self-esteem in single and two parented homes. *American Sociological Association (ASA)*.

Dail, P. W. (1993). Homeless in America: Involuntary family migration. *Marriage and Family Review, 19*(1-2), 55-75.

Dail, P. W. (1990). The psychological context of homeless mothers with young children: Program and policy implications. Child Welfare League of America, 0009-4021/90/040291-18.

D'Ercole, A., and Struening, E. (1987). *Predictors of depression among homeless women: Implications for service delivery*. Paper presented at the American Orthopsychiatric Association Annual Program Meetings, Washington, D.C.

Dickstein, E. B., and Posner, J. M. (1978). Self-esteem and relationship with parents. *Journal of Genetic Psychology, 133*(2), 273-276.

Dornbusch, S. M. (1994). Additional perspectives on homeless families. *American Behavioral Scientist, 37*(3), 404-411.

Downer, R. T. (1996). Separation and rejoining behaviors of homeless and housed low-income parents and their children in child care settings. Unpublished manuscript.

Dumas, J. E. (1986). Indirect influence of maternal social contacts on mother-child interactions: A setting event analysis. *Journal of Abnormal Child Psychology, 14*, 205-216.

Dunst, C., Jenkins, V., and Trivette, C. (1984). The Family Support Scale: Reliability and validity. *Journal of Individual, Family, and Community Wellness, 1*(4), 45-52.

Dyson, J. L. (1990). The effects of family violence on children's academic performance and behavior. *Journal of the National Medical Association, 82*(1), 17-22.

Edell, B. H., and Motta, R. W. (1989). The emotional adjustment of children with Tourette's syndrome. *Journal of Psychology, 123*(1), 51-57.

Edelstein, R. I. (1972). Early intervention in the poverty cycle. *Social Casework, 53*, 418-424.

Elliot, G. R., and Eisdorfer, C. (Eds.). (1982). Stress and human health: Analysis and implication of research. New York: Springer.

Eyberg, S. M., Boggs, S. R., and Rodriguez, C. M. (1992). Relationships between maternal parenting stress and child descriptive behavior. *Child and Family Behavior Therapy,* 14(4), 1-9.

Feldman, H. and Feldman, M. (1979). The effect of father absence on adolescents. *Family Perspective, 10,* 13-16.

Fischer, P. J. (1991). *Alcohol, drug abuse and mental health problems among homeless persons: A review of the literature, 1980-1990.* Rockville, MD: National Institute on Alcohol Abuse and Alcoholism and National Institute of Mental Health.

Fischer, P. J., and Breakey, W. R. (1987). Profile of the Baltimore homeless with alcohol problems. *Alcohol Health and Research World,* 11(3), 36-41.

Freden, L. (1982). *Psychological aspects of depression: No way out?* New York: Wiley.

Garmezy, N., Masten, A. S., and Tellegen, A. (1984). The study of stress and competence in children: A building block for developing psychopathology. *Child Development, 55,* 97-111.

Ge, X., Conger, R. D., and Elder, G. H. (1992). Linking family economic hardship to adolescent distress. *Journal of Research and Adolescence,* 2(4), 351-378.

Ge, X., Conger, R. D., Lorenz, F. O., and Simons, R. L. (1994). Parents' stressful life events and adolescent depressed mood. *Journal of Health and Social Behavior,* 35(1)28-44.

Geanotti, T. J., and Doyle, R. E. (1982). The effectiveness of parental training on learning disabled children and their parents. *Elementary School Guidance and Counseling, 17,* 131-136.

Gecas, V. (1979). The influence of social class on socialization. In W. R. Burr, R. Hill, F. I. Nye, and I. L. Reiss (Eds.), *Contemporary theories about the family, 1,* 365-404. New York: Free Press.

Gelles, R. J., and Straus, M. A. (1979). Violence in the American family. *Journal of Social Issues, 35,* 15-39.

Giannotti, T. J., and Doyle, R. F. (1982). The effectiveness of parental training on learning disabled children and their parents. *Elementary School Guidance and Counseling,* 17(2), 131-136.

Gold, S. R., Milan, L. D., Mayall, A., and Johnson, A. E. (1994). A cross-validation-study of the traumatic symptom checklist: The role of mediating variables. *Journal of Interpersonal Violence,* 39(1), 12-26.

Goodman, S. H., Adamson, L. B., Riniti, J., and Cole, S. (1994). Mothers' expressed attitudes: Associations with maternal depression and children's self-esteem and psychopathology. *Journal of the American Academy of Child and Adolescent Psychiatry, 33*(9), 1265-1274.

Gory, M., Ritchey, F. J., and Fitzpatrick, K. (1991). Homelessness and affiliation. *Sociological Quarterly, 32*(2), 201-218.

Grant, R. (1990). The special needs of homeless children. Early intervention at a welfare hotel. *Topics in Early Childhood Special Education, 10*(4), 76-91.

Graybill, D. (1978). Relationship of maternal child-rearing behaviors to children's self-esteem. *Journal of Psychology, 100*(1), 45-47.

Hagen, J. L., and Ivanoff, A. M. (1988). Homeless women: A high risk population. *Affilia, 3*(2), 19-33.

Hall, J. A., and Maza, P. (1990). No fixed address: The effects of homelessness on families and children. *Child and Youth Services, 14*(1), 35-47.

Hashima, P. Y., and Amato, P. R. (1994). Poverty, social support, and parental behavior. *Child Development, 65*, 394-403.

Hausman, B., and Hammen, C. (1993). Parenting in homeless families: The double crisis. *American Journal of Orthopsychiatry, 63*(3), 358-369.

Hazzard, A, Christensen, A., and Margolin, G. (1983). Children's perceptions of parental behaviors. *Journal of Abnormal Child Psychology, 11*(1), 49-59.

Hodges, W. F., Tierney, C. W., and Buchsbaum, H. K. (1984). The cumulative effects of stress on preschool children of divorced and intact families. *Journal of Marriage and the Family, 46*(3), 611-617.

Homes for the Homeless. (1992). Who are homeless families? A profile of homelessness in New York City.

Hue, P. T. (1979). An investigation of the relationship between adolescents' self-esteem, perceived parent-child communication satisfaction, and feelings toward parents. Unpublished doctoral dissertation, University of Houston.

Hunter, R. S., and Kilstrom, N. (1979). Breaking the cycle in abusive families. *American Journal of Psychiatry, 136*, 1320-1322.

Huttman, E., and Redmond, S. (1992). Women and homelessness: Evidence of need to look beyond shelters to long term social services assistance and permanent housing. *Journal of Sociology and Social Welfare, 19*(4), 89-111.

Jennings, K. D., Stagg, V., and Connors, R. E. (1991). Social networks and mothers' interactions with their preschool children. *Child Development, 62*, 966-978.

Justice, B., Calvert, A., and Justice, R. (1985). Factors mediating child abuse as a response to stress. *Child Abuse and Neglect, 9*, 359-363.

Kanner, A. D., Coyne, J. C., Schafer, C., and Lazarus, R. S. (1981). Comparisons of two models of stress measurement: Daily hassles and uplift versus major life events. *Journal of Behavioral Medicine, 4*, 1-39.

Kaslow, F. W., and Cooper, B. (1978). Family therapy with the learning disabled child and his/her family. *Journal of Marriage and Family Therapy, 4*(1), 41-49.

Kelley, M. L., Power, T. G., and Wimbush, D. D. (1992). Determinants of disciplinary practices in low-income black mothers. *Child Development, 63*(3), 573-582.

Kelly, T., Sheldon, S., and Fox, G. (1985). The impact of economic dislocation on the health of children. In J. Boulet, A. M. Debritto, and S. A. Ray (Eds.) *The impact of poverty and unemployment on children*, pp. 94-108. Ann Arbor, MI: University of Michigan, Bush Program in Child Development and Social Policy.

Kids Count Data Online. (1999). The Annie E. Casey Foundation.

Kiester, D. J. (1973). Who am I? The development of self-concept. Durham, N.C.: Learning Institute of North Carolina.

Killeen, M. R. (1993). Parent influences on children's self-esteem in economically disadvantaged families. *Issues in Mental Health Nursing, 14*(4), 323-336.

Kinzel, D. M. (1993). Response to "The meaning of being homeless." *Scholarly Enquiry for Nursing Practice, 7*(1), 71-73.

Kissman, K. (1988). Factors associated with competence and parenting attitudes among teen mothers. *International Journal of Adolescence and Youth, 1*(3), 247-255.

Knickman, J. R., and Weitzman, B. C. (1989). *A study of homeless families in New York City: Final report.* Volumes 2 and 3. New York: New York University Health Research Program.

Kobe, F. H. (1994). Parenting stress and depression in children with mental retardation and developmental disabilities. *Research in Developmental Disabilities, 15*(3), 209-221.

Koblinsky, S. A., and Anderson, E. A. (1993a). *Family functioning and child development in homeless and housed Head Start families.* Paper presented at the 2nd National Head Start Research Conference, Washington, D.C.

Koeske, G. F., and Koeske, R. D. (1990). The buffering effect of social support on parental stress. *American Journal of Orthopsychiatry, 60*(3), 440-668.

Kondratas, S. A. (1991). Ending homelessness: Policy challenges. *American Psychologist, 46,* 1226-1231.

Kotch, J. B., and Thomas, L. P. (1986). Family and social factors associated with substantiation of child abuse and neglect reports. *Journal of Family Violence, 1,* 167-179.

Kotlowitz, A. (1991). *There are no children here.* New York: Doubleday.

Krugman, R. D., Lenherr, M., Betz, L., and Fryer, G. E. (1986). The relationship between unemployment and physical abuse of children. *Child Abuse and Neglect, 10,* 415-418.

Kurtz, L. (1994). Psychosocial coping resources in elementary school-age children of divorce. *American Journal of Orthopsychiatry, 64*(40), 554-563.

Landers, S. (1989). Homeless children lose childhood. *American Psychological Association Monitor,* pp. 1-33.

Lawson, K. A., and Hays, J. R. (1989). Self-esteem and stress as factors in abuse of children. *Psychological Reports, 65*(3), 1259-1265.

Lazarus, R. S. (1984). Puzzles in the study of daily hassles. *Journal of Behavioral Medicine, 7, 375-389.*

Lazarus, R. S., Cohen, J. B., Folkman, S., Kanner, A., and Schaefer, C. (1980). Psychological stress and adaptation: Some unresolved issues. In J. Selye (Ed.), *Selye's guide to stress research,* (vol. 1, pp. 90-117). New York: Van Nostrand Reinhold.

Leadbeater, B. J., and Bishop, S. J. (1994). Predictors of behavior problems in preschool children of inner-city Afro-American and Puerto Rican adolescent mothers. *Child Development, 65*(2), 638-648.

Lee, C. M., and Gotlib, I. H. (1989). Clinical status and emotional adjustment of children of depressed mothers. *American Journal of Psychiatry, 146*(4), 478-483.

Letiecq, B. L., Anderson, E. A., and Koblinsky, S. A. (1996). Social support of homeless and permanently housed low-income mothers with young children. *Journal of Family Relations, 45,* 265-272.

Liebow, E. (1993). *Tell them who I am: The lives of homeless women.* New York: Free Press.

Lifshitz, M. (1975). Social differentiation and organization of the Rorchach in fatherless and two parented children. *Journal of Clinical Psychology, 31*, 126-130.

Longfellow, C., Zelkowitz, P., and Saunders, E. (1982). The quality of mother-child relationships. In D. Belle (Ed.), *Lives in stress: Women and depression* (pp. 163-176). Beverly Hills, CA: Sage.

Lorion, R. P., and Saltzman, W. (1993). Children's exposure to community violence: Following a path from concern to research to action. *Psychiatry, 56*, 55-65.

Mahabeer, M. (1993). Correlations between mothers' and children's self-esteem and perceived familial relationships among intact, widowed, and divorced families. *Psychological Reports, 73*(2), 483-489.

Markus, H., Crane, M., Bernstein, S., and Siladi, M. (1982). Self-schemas and gender. *Journal of Personality and Social Psychology, 42*(1), 38-50.

Mash, E. J., and Johnston, C. (1983). Parental perceptions of child behavior problem, parenting self-esteem, and mothers' reported stress in younger and older hyperactive and normal children. *Journal of Consulting Psychology, 51*, 86-99.

Maslow, A. H. (1954). *Motivation and personality*. New York: Harper and Row.

Masten, A. S. (1992). Homeless children in the United States: Mark of a nation at risk. *Current Direction In Psychological Science, 1*(2), 41-44.

Maza, P. L., and Hall, J. A. (1988). *Homeless children and their families*: A preliminary study. Washington, D.C: Child Welfare League of America.

McChesney, K. Y. (1986a). Families: The new homeless. *Family Professional, 1*(2), 6-7.

McChesney, K. Y. (1986b). New findings on homeless families. *Family Professional, 1*(2), 19-27.

McCormick, L., and Holden, R. (1992). Homeless children a special challenge. *Young Children, 47*, 61-67.

McCullough, P. M., Ashbridge, D., and Pegg, R. (1994). The effect of self-esteem, family structure, locus of control, and career goals on adolescent leadership behavior. *Adolescence, 29*(1), 605-611.

McLeod, J. D., Kruttschnitt, C., and Dornfell, M. (1994). Does parenting explain effects of structural conditions on children's antisocial behavior? A comparison of blacks and whites. *Social Forces, 73*(2), 574-604.

McLoyd, V. C. (1990). The impact of economic hardship on black families and children: Psychological distress, parenting, and socioeconomic development. *Child Development, 61*, 311-346.

McLoyd, V. C., and Wilson, L. (1991). The strain of living poor: Parenting social support, and child mental health. In A. C. Huston. *Children in Poverty*. (Chapter 5). Cambridge University Press.

Mead, G. H. (1934). *Mind, self, and society*. Chicago: University of Chicago Press.

Melnick, V. L., and Williams, C. S. (1987). *Children and families without homes: observations from thirty cases*. Washington: University of the District of Columbia, Center for Applied Research and Urban Policy.

Miller, D., S., and Lin, E. H. B. (1988) Children in sheltered homeless families: Reported health status and use of health services. *Pediatrics, 81*, 668-673.

Mills, C., and Ota, H. (1989). Homeless women with minor children in Detroit metropolitan area. *Social Work, 34*(6), 485-489.

Mirowsky, J., and Ross, C. E. (1983). Paranoia and the structure of powerlessness. *American Sociological Review, 48*, 228-239.

Molnar, J. (1988). *Home is where the heart is: The crisis of homeless children and families in New York City*. New York: Bank Street College of Education.

Molnar, J. M., Rath, R. R., and Klein, T. P. (1990). Constantly compromised: The impact of homelessness on children. *Journal of Social Issues, 46*(4), 109-124.

Moos, R. H., Clayton, J., and Max, W. (1979). *The social climate scales: An annotated bibliography*. Palo Alto, CA: Consulting Psychologists Press.

Moos, R. H., and Moos, B. (1981). *Revised Family Environment Scale*. Palo Alto, CA: Consulting Psychology Press.

Moos, R. H., and Moos, B. S. (1994). *A social climate. Family Environment Scale manual*. Center for Health Care Evaluations, Department of Veterans Affairs and Stanford University Medical Centers. Palo Alto, California.

Moos, R. H., and Spinard, S. (1984). The social climate scales: An annotated bibliography. Palo Alto, CA: Consulting Psychologists Press.

Morvitz, E. and Motta, R. (1992). Predictors of self-esteem: The roles of parent-child perceptions, achievement, and class placement. *Journal of Learning Disabilities, 25*(1), 72-80.

National Coalition for the Homeless. (1987). *Broken lives: Denial of education to homeless children.* Washington, D.C.: Author.

National Commission on Children (U.S). (1991). *Beyond rhetoric: A new American agenda for children and families.* Library of Congress Cataloging-in-Publication Data.

Nelson, G. (1993). Risk, resistance, and self-esteem: A longitudinal study of elementary school-aged children from mother custody and two-parent families. *Journal of Divorce and Remarriage, 19*(1-2), 99-119.

Newberger, E. H., Hampton, R. L., Marx, T. J., and White, K. M. (1986). Child abuse and pediatric social illness: An epidemiological analysis and ecological reformation. *American Journal of Orthopsychiatry, 56*(4), 589-601.

Nolan, S. M. (1987). Relationship of child's self-concept, perception of parent's attitude toward child, and academic achievement. Unpublished doctoral dissertation. Hofstra University, Hampstead, NY.

Nunn, G. D., and Parish, T. (1987). An investigation of the relationships between children's self-concepts and evaluations of parent figures: Do they vary as a function of family structure? *Journal of Psychology, 121*(6), 563-566.

Oates, R. K. (1986). The causes of child abuse. In *Child abuse and neglect: What happens eventually?* (Chapter 5). New York: Brunner/Mazel.

Omizo, M. M., Amerikaner, M. J., and Michael, W. B. (1985). The Coopersmith Self-esteem Inventory as a predictor of feelings and communication satisfaction toward parents among learning disabled, emotionally disturbed, and normal adolescents. *Educational and Psychological Measurement, 45*, 389-395.

Parish, T. S., and Copeland, T. (1979). The relationship between self-concepts and evaluations of parents and stepfathers. *Journal of Psychology, 101*, 135-138.

Parish, T. S., and Dostal, J. W. (1980). Relationships between evaluations of self and parents by children from intact and divorced families. *Journal of Psychology, 104*, 35-38.

Parish, T. S., and McCluskey, J. J. (1994). The relationships between parenting styles and young adults' self-concepts and evaluations of parents. *Family Therapy, 21*(3), 223-226.

Parks, P. L., Lenz, E. R., and Jenkins, L. S. (1992). The role of social support and stressors for mothers and infants. *Child Care Health and Development, 18*(3), 151-171.

Patterson, G. (1988). Stress: A change agent for family process. In N. Garmezy and M. Rutter (Eds.). *Stress Coping and Development in Children*, (pp. 235-264). Baltimore: Johns Hopkins University Press.

Patterson, G., DeBarsyshe, B., and Ramsey, E. (1989). A developmental perspective on antisocial behavior. *American Psychologist, 44*, 329-335.

Pelton, L. H. (1981). *The social context of child abuse and neglect*. New York: Human Sciences press.

Pianta, R. C., and Egeland, B. (1990). Life stress and parenting outcomes in a disadvantaged sample: Results of the Mother-Child Interaction Project. *Journal of Clinical Child Psychology, 19*(4), 329-336.

Piers, E. V., and Harris, D. B. (1969). *The Piers-Harris Children's Self-concept Scale. Revised Manual*. Western Psychological Services. Los Angeles, California.

Power, T. G. (1989). *The Parenting Dimensions Inventory*. Unpublished manuscript, University of Houston.

Rafferty, Y., and Rollins, N. (1989). *Learning in limbo: The educational deprivation of homeless children*. New York: Advocates for Children of New York.

Rafferty, Y., and Shinn, M. (1991). The impact of homeless on children. *American Psychologist, 46*(11), 1170-1179.

Raschke, H. J., and Raschke, V. J. (1979). Family conflict and children's self-concept: A comparison of intact and single-parent families. *Journal of Marriage and the Family, 41*, 367-374.

Reid, J. B., and Kavanagh, K. (1985). A social interactional approach to child abuse: Risk, prevention, and treatment. In M. Chesney and R. Rosenman (Eds.). *Anger and Hostility in Behavioral and Cardiovascular Disorders*. (Chapter 13). New York: Hemisphere/McGraw-Hill.

Rescorla, L., Parker, R., and Stolley, P. (1991). Ability, achievement, and adjustment in homeless children. *American Journal of Orthopsychiatry, 61*(2), 210-220.

Richters, J. E. (1993). Community violence and children's development: Toward a research agenda for the 1990s. *Psychiatry, 56*, 3-6.

Rivlin, L. G. (1990). Home and homelessness in the lives of children. *Child and Youth Services, 14*(1), 5-17.

Roberts, L., and Henry, M. (1986). State ordered to shelter homeless families. *Youth Law News, 7*(4), 1-3.

Rodgers, A. Y. (1993). The assessment of variables related to the parenting behavior of mothers with young children. *Child and Youth Services Review, 15*(5), 385-402.

Roggman, L. A., Moe, S. T., Hart, A. D., and Forthun, L. F. (1994). Family leisure and social support: Relations with parenting stress and psychological well-being in head start parents. *Early Childhood Research Quarterly, 9*(3-4), 463-480.

Roopnavine, J. L., Church, C. C., and, Levy, G. D. (1990). Day care children's play behaviors, marital stress, and marital companionship. *Early Childhood Research Quarterly, 5*(3), 335-346.

Rossi, P. H. (1994). Troubling families: Family homelessness in America. *American Behavioral Scientist, 37*(3), 342-395.

Rossi, P. H. (1990). The old homeless and the new homeless in historical perspective. *American Psychologist, 45*(8), 954-959.

Sailor, P., and Crumley, W. (1975). Self image: How do the poor see themselves? *Journal of Home Economics, 67,* 4-8.

Salzinger, S., Kaplan, S., and Artemyeff, C. (1983). Mothers' personal social networks and child maltreatment. *Journal of Abnormal Psychology, 92,* 66-76.

Sameroff, A. J., and Seifer, R. (1983). Familial risk and child competence. *Child Development, 54*(5), 1254-1268.

Schubert, H. J. P. (1935). *Twenty thousand transients: A year's sample of those who apply for aid in an northern city.* Buffalo, NY: Emergency Relief Bureau.

Schweitzer, R. D., Hier, S. T., and Terry, D. J. (1994). Parental bonding, family systems, and environmental predictions of adolescent homelessness. *Journal of Emotional and Behavioral Disorders, 2*(1), 39-45.

Scott, W. A., Scott, R., and McCabe, M. (1991). Family relationships and children's personality: A cross-cultural cross-source comparison. *British Journal of Social Psychology, 30*(1), 1-20.

Seagull, E. A. W. (1987). Social support and child maltreatment: A review of the evidence. *Child Abuse and Neglect, 11*(1), 41-52.

Shere, P. (1992). *Who are homeless families? A profile of homelessness in New York City.* Homes for the Homeless, Inc., New York, NY. Institute for Poverty, New York, NY.

Slater, M. A., and Power, T. G. (1987). Multidimensional assessment of parenting in single-parent families. In J. P. Vincent (Ed.), *Advances in family intervention, assessment, and theory.* pp. 197-228. Greenwich, CN: JAI Press.

Snow, D. A., and Anderson, L. (1993). Down on their luck: A study of homeless street people. Berkley: University of California Press.

Solarz, A., and Bogat, G. A. (1990). When social supports fail: The homeless. *Journal of Community Psychology, 18*(1), 79-96.

Spivak, G., and Shure, M. (1974). *Social adjustment of young children.* San Francisco: Josey Bass.

Stark, L. R. (1994). The shelter as "total institution": An organizational barrier to remedying homelessness. *American Behavioral Scientist, 37*(4), 553-562.

Steinberg, L., Catalano, R., and Dooley, D. (1981). Economic antecedents of child abuse and neglect. *Child Development, 52*, 975-986.

Stoneman, Z., Brody, G. H., and Burke, M. (1989). Marital quality, depression, and inconsistent parenting: Relationship with observed mother-child conflict. *American Journal of Orthopsychiatry, 59*(1), 105-117.

Straus, M. A. (1980). Stress and physical child abuse. *Child Abuse and Neglect, 4*, 75-88.

Sullivan, H. S. (1945). *Conceptions of modern psychiatry.* Washington, D.C.: The William Alanson White Psychiatric Foundation.

Summerlin, M. I. (1978). The effects of parental participation in a parent group on a child's self-concept. *Journal of Psychology, 100*(2), 227-232.

Thomas, D. L., Gecas, V., Weigert, A., and Rooney, E. (1974). *Family socialization and the adolescent.* Lexington, MA: D.C. Heath.

Tocco, T. S., and Bridges, C. M. (1973). The relationship between the self-concepts of mothers and their children. *Child Study Journal, 3*, 61-79.

U.S. Conference of Mayors. (1993). *A status report on hunger and homelessness in American cities: A 26 City Survey.* Washington, D.C.

U.S. Department of Commerce, Bureau of the Census, Current Population Reports. (1989). *School enrollment - social and economic characteristics of students.* Washington, D.C.: Government Printing Office, 1990. p.7.

U.S. Department of Commerce, Bureau of the Census, Current Population Reports. (1989). *School enrollment - social and economic characteristics of* students. Washington, D.C.: Government Printing Office, 1990. p.65.

U.S. Department of Commerce, Bureau of the Census, Current Population Reports. (1989). *School enrollment - social and economic characteristics of students*. Washington, D.C.: Government Printing Office, 1990. p.66.

U.S. Department of Education. (1989). *Report to the Congress on State interim reports on the education of homeless children*. Washington, D.C: Author.

U.S. Congress, House of Representatives, Select Committee on Children, Youth and Families. (1987). *No place to call home*. Washington, D.C.: Government Printing Office, 1988. p.66.

Wagner, J. K., and Perrine, R. M. (1994). Women at risk for homelessness: Comparison between housed and homeless women. *Psychological Reports, 75*, 1671-1678.

Webster-Stratton, C., Kolpacoff, M., and Hollinsworth, T. (1988). Self-administered videotape therapy for families with conduct problem children: Comparison with two cost effective treatments and a control group. *Journal of Consulting and Clinical Psychology, 56*(4), 558-566.

Weinraub, M., and Wolf, B. (1983). Effects of stress and social supports on mother-child interactions in single and two-parent families. *Child Development, 54*, 1297-1311.

Weitzman, B. C., Knickman, J. R., and Shinn, M. (1990). Pathways to homelessness among New York City families. *Journal of Social Issues, 46*(4), 125-140.

Werner, E. E., and Smith, R. S. (1982). *Vulnerable but invincible: A longitudinal study of resilient children and youth* New York: McGraw Hill.

Whipple, E. E., and Webster-Stratton, C. (1991). The role of parental stress in physical abuse families. *Child Abuse and Neglect, 15*, 279-291.

Whitman, B. Y., Accardo, P., Boyert, M., and Kendagor, R. (1990). Homelessness and cognitive performance in children: A possible link. *National Association of Social Workers, Inc.* CCC Code: 0037-8046.

Whitman, B. Y., Stretch, J., and Accardo, P. (1987). Testimony presented before the U.S. House of Representatives select committee on Children, Youth, and Families. The Crisis of Homelessness: Effects on Children and Families (p.125). Washington, D.C. U.S. Government Printing Office.

Winkleby, M, A. (1990). Comparison of risk factors for ill health in a sample of homeless poor. *American Journal of Public Health, 80*(9), 1049-1052.

Wood, D., Valdez, R. B., Hayashi, T., and Shen, A. (1990). Homeless and housed families in Los Angeles: A study comparing demographic, economic and family functioning characteristics. *American Journal of Public Health, 80,* 1049-1052.

Wolock, I., and Horowitz, B. (1979). Child maltreatment and material deprivation among AFDC-recipient families. *Social Service Review, 53,* 175-194.

Wright, J. (1987). Effect of homelessness on the psychological well-being of children, families, and youth. National evaluation of the Johnson-Pew "Health Care for the Homeless" Program.

Wright, J. D. (1991). Health and the homeless teenager: Evidence from the National Health Care for the Homeless Program. Special Issue: Homeless and runaway youth. *Journal of Health and Social Policy,* 2(4), 15-35.

Wright, J. D. (1990). Poor people, poor health: The health status of the homeless. *Journal of Social Issues,* 46(4), 49-64.

Wylie, R. (1961). The self-concept, a critical survey of pertinent research literature. Lincoln, Nebraska: University of Nebraska Press.

Zeisemer, C., Marcoux, L., and Marwell, B, E. (1994). "Homeless children: Are they different from other low-income children?" *Social Work,* 39(6), 658-668.

Ziefert, M., and Strauch-Brown, K. (1991). Skill building for effective intervention with homeless families. *Families in Society: The Journal of Contemporary Human Services, 73,* 212-219.

Zina, B. T., Wells, K. B., and Freeman, H. E. (1994). Emotional and behavioral problems and severe academic delays among sheltered homeless children in Los Angeles County. *American Journal of Public Health,* 84(2), 260-264.

Subject Index

Abuse:
    alcohol, 3, 6
    child, 6, 11–12, 14–15
    drug, 3
    physical, 3, 6
    sexual, 3, 6–7
    substance, 6, 7, 11
Academic performance, 20
Adolescents, 11
Aggression, 17–19
Anxiety, 11–12, 17–18, 29, 38, 51, 66, 74, 87, 92

Battering, 3, 6
Behavioral problems, 17, 19, 28–29, 31–33, 51–53, 61–63, 82–83, 87–88, 90
    children's, 64
    externalizing, 29, 37, 51–53, 65–66, 73–74, 77, 82–85
    homeless children, 31
    internalizing, 37, 51–53, 65–69, 83, 87

Child:
    abuse, 6, 12, 14–15
    behavior checklist, 37, 39–40
    neglect, 5–6
    psychopathology, 13
Cognitive, 23–24

Demographic:
    conditions, 21
    data, 31–32, 45
    homeless families, 1, 17, 47–48
    homeless group, 43–44
    homeless population, 2
    homeless preschoolers, 17
Depressed, 10–11
    moods, 12
    mothers, 25
Depression, 12
Discipline, 10, 12
Distress, psychological, 9–10
Domestic violence, 6–7
Domiciled:
    children, 18
    disadvantaged children, 19
    peers, 19
    poor, 3
    students, 20
Drugs, maternal, 3

Economic:
    hardship, 5, 6, 9
    loss, 10
Education, 2, 3, 5, 9, 11–12, 19, 29, 45, 78, 91
Emotional:
    problems, 19, 29
    stability, 27
Employment, 1, 5–6, 11–12, 29, 43, 45, 78
    special, 19–20

Family:
    climate, 28
    conflict, 27–28, 86
    discord, 4–5
    divorced, 24
    environment scale, 35, 39–40, 81
    functioning, 13, 27, 46, 77, 80, 86, 87
    harmony, 28
    intact, 24
    interaction, 27
    low-income, 4, 31, 80, 90
    mother headed, 28
    process, 25, 80–81, 87
    process variables, 88
    quality, 28
    shelters, 17
    single parent, 27–28, 85
    structure, 1, 27–28
    support scale, 33–34, 39–40
Fear, 11

Guilt, 10–11, 29

Hassles, 13
    daily, 13–14
    parenting, 14
Head Start, 14–15, 79
Health:
    problems, 15, 18
    risks, 15
    status of homeless children, 15
Homeless:
    adults, 5
    boys, 83
    children, 1, 4–5, 15–19, 23–25, 32, 43–46, 77–83, 85,87, 52, 84
    depression era, 1
    families, 1–5, 20, 31–32, 43, 46–47, 77–79, 89–90, 48, 74, 89
    females, 15, 44
    girls, 83
    men, 7, 2
    mothers, 6, 12, 32, 81
    new, 1,12
    old, 1, 2
    parent, 4–5, 9, 25, 77,82
    population, 2
    students, 20
Housed:
    at-risk, 6
    children, 16, 19, 43, 49, 82–84, 87, 90
    families, 43, 89–90
    mothers, 6, 12, 32
    parents, 25
    poor children, 16
    poor women, 15
    low-income, 20, 31
    subsidized, 3
    unstable, 89
Housing, 4, 5
    crisis, 5
    crowded, 3
    doubled-up, 44, 45
    inadequate, 12
    low-cost, 4
    low-income, 31
    permanent, 4
    public, 15, 3

Subject Index

Hypotheses, 31

Income, 12
  limited, 12
  low, 14
  family, 16
Interpersonal relationships, 6, 31–33, 35, 40, 47, 64, 66–73, 77, 80–81, 86–88, 89–91

Life events, stressful, 11–13

Marital discord, 11
Motel, 5, 32, 89

Outcomes:
  physical, 4
  cognitive, 4
  social, 4

Parent:
  behavior, 12–14
  child relationship, 11–13, 25–26, 82–84, 85–90, 92
  control, 36, 48, 86–87
  functioning, 13, 15
  homeless, 7–9, 25–26
  influence on children's self-concept, 23
  low-income, 82
  psychopathology symptomatology, 12–14
  single, 2, 24, 85
  social network, 88
  structure, 36
  symptomatology, 14
  system, 13
  teen, 5
Parenting, 4, 9
  ability, 25
  control, 88
  behavior, 13–14, 28
  dimensions, 36
  dimensions inventory, 36, 39–40, 82
  hassles, 82
  inconsistent, 28, 40
  interdimensional model, 37
  nurturance, 40
  practices, 87
  process, 12
  quality, 4, 6, 31–33, 36, 40, 47–48, 64, 66–73, 77, 82–83, 87–89
  role, 19–20, 87
  stress, 82
  structure, 48, 66–73, 87
  style, 26
  support, 40, 48, 66–73, 87
Personal:
  growth, 31–33, 35, 40, 47, 64, 66–73, 75, 86–90
  functioning, 90
Piers-Harris Children's Self-concept Scale, 38–40, 48
Poverty, 2–5, 9–12, 16, 25–26, 29, 78, 81, 89
Preschoolers, 4, 12, 17–19
Process resources, 31–33, 81
Psychological distress, 9–10, 12

Self-concept, 23–24, 26, 29, 31–33, 38, 48, 49–51, 53–60, 64–67, 70–75, 77, 83, 86–88, 92
  children's, 23–28, 87, 90
  college students, 24
  global, 52, 74–75, 77, 83
  homeless children, 23, 26, 31–32, 82–83
  impaired, 26
  income, 12
  mothers', 25
  negative, 26–28
  parent, 24, 27

poor, 26
positive, 28
Self-esteem, 26, 29, 91
  children's, 25–27
  low, 27
  maternal, 4
  parents', 14, 25
Shelter, 2, 5,9–11, 13, 20, 25, 32, 38–39, 78, 80–83, 87, 89–92
  rules, 82, 85–86, 90–91
Social, 3, 7, 10, 14–15, 28–29, 31, 47–48, 79–80
  connections, 11
  development, 24
  embeddedness questionnaire, 35, 40, 47
  experiences, 7, 23–25
  identification, 24
  interactions, 7, 9
  relations, 25
  skills, 4
Socioeconomic status, 15, 18–20, 27
Stigma, 24
Stress, 4, 7, 9–10, 12, 13, 90
  a mediator, 12
  chronic, 14
  daily, 13
  families in, 14
  family, 7
  maternal, 14
  parental, 14–15, 29
  parenting, 12–14
  reported by mothers, 29
  sources of, 12
Support:
  embeddedness, 33–35, 80
  emotional, 12
  enacted, 33–35, 80
  family, 27, 31
  formal, 31, 34, 40
  informal, 31
  mothers' social, 14

  parental, 36, 86, 87
  perceived, 33–35, 80
  social, 3, 7, 10, 14–15, 28–29, 31–33, 47–48, 79–80, 90
  systems, 3

Unemployment, 11, 12, 78

Welfare, 2, 25
  child, 5
  department, 2
  hotels, 15, 16
Well-being, children's psychological, 14–15
Women:
  homeless, 3, 6, 7
  housed, 6
  poor, 25
  single, 3

Name Index

Aber, 82
Abidin, 12
Achenbach, 37-38
Alperstein, 15-16
Altman, 27
Amato, 14
Amerikaner, 26
Anderson, 7, 12, 78, 82
Arnstein, 16
Artemyeff, 14

Bahr, 2
Barrera, 33
Basham, 13
Bassuk, 3, 6-7, 16-20, 78, 80-83
Bauman, 11-12, 82, 84, 85
Beaty, 80-82, 85
Beckman, 13
Belle, 12
Belsky, 12
Bernstein, 16
Biedel, 89
Bishop, 29
Blumberg, 2
Boe, 7
Bogart, 15
Bogue, 2
Booth, 85

Bourgois, 80
Boxill, 80-82, 85
Braddock, 29
Braithwaite, 27
Breakey, 7
Brody, 28
Bronfenbrenner, 9-10
Buchsbaum, 88
Burke, 28

Calsyn, 27
Caplow, 2
Catalone, 12
Christensen, 26
Church, 29
Cohen, 13
Conger, 11, 12
Connell, 82
Connors, 14
Cooley-Quille, 89
Cooper, 27
Corse, 14
Coyne, 13
Creasey, 29
Crinic, 13, 14
Crystal, 7
Cuers, 29

Dadds, 29
Dager, 27
Dail, 2
DeBarsyshe, 10
Demas, 13
D'Ercole, 7
Dooley, 12
Dornbusch, 3-4, 7, 14, 79
Doyle, 26
Dunst, 33-34
Dyson, 83, 85

Edelbrock, 37
Edell, 26
Edelstein, 89
Elliot, 29

Feldman, 28
Firnesz, 27
Fisher, 7
Flanigan, 15
Folkman, 13
Forthum, 15
Fox, 35, 86

Gallagher, 80
Garmezy, 12
Ge, 11
Gecas, 36
Gelles, 14
Gianotti, 26
Gold, 88
Gounis, 82
Grant, 17
Graybill, 26
Greca, 10
Green, 35
Greenberg, 13, 14

Hagen, 7, 81
Hall, 19, 78
Harowitz, 14

Harris, 27, 38
Hart, 15
Hashima, 14
Hayashi, 16
Hazzard, 26
Henry, 15
Hier, 11
Higgins, 85
Hodges, 88
Holden, 4
Hollinsworth, 28
Holman, 27
Hunter, 14
Huttman, 11

Ivanoff, 7, 81

Jarvis, 29
Jenkins, 14, 33-34
Jennings, 14
Johnson, 13, 85, 88

Kanner, 13
Kaplan, 14
Kaslow, 27
Kelly, 36, 86
Killeen, 29
Kilstrom, 14
Kinzel, 11
Klein, 19
Knickman, 5
Koblinsky, 12, 78
Koeske, 14
Kolpacoff, 28
Kondratas, 2
Kotch, 14
Kropp, 12

Lahey, 12
Landers, 18
Lauriat, 7
Lazarus, 13

Name Index

Leadbeater, 29
Lenz, 14
Letiecq, 3, 34-35, 79-80
Levy, 29
Liebow, 82
Linn, 15
Lorenz, 11
Lorion, 82, 88

Mackbin, 35
Margolin, 26
Martin, 89
Mash, 13
Maslow, 9, 79
Masten, 12
Master, 89
Mayhall, 88
Max, 35
Maza, 19, 78
McCarthy, 12
McCormick, 4
McHesney, 4
McLoyd, 9-10, 13, 81-82, 84, 89
Mian, 88
Michael, 26
Miller, 15
Mills, 81
Moe, 15
Molnar, 19
Moos, 35
Morgan, 12
Motta, 26

Nolan, 26

Omizo, 26-27
Otta, 81

Parker, 19
Parks, 14
Patterson, 10, 13
Pelton, 12

Pervine, 6, 78
Piers, 38
Power, 36

Quicke, 27

Rafferty, 15, 19-20, 78, 85
Ramsey, 10
Rappalation, 15
Raschke, 13, 27-28
Rath, 19
Redmond, 11
Regozin, 13
Rescorla, 19, 21, 82
Richards, 85
Roberts, 15
Robinson, 13
Rodgers, 13, 14
Rodriquez, 83, 85
Roggman, 15
Rollins, 19-20, 78
Rooney, 36
Roopnavine, 29
Rosenberg, 3, 6-7, 17-18, 20, 78, 81, 83
Rossi, 1
Rotation, 35
Rubin, 7, 17, 19-20

Salinzer, 14
Saltzman, 82, 88
Sameroff, 13
Schafer, 13
Schmidt, 14
Schweitzer, 11
Seifer, 13
Shellman, 86
Shinn, 5, 15-16, 85
Shure, 27
Slater, 36
Smith, 7, 12
Snow, 82

Solarz, 15
Spence, 82
Spinard, 35
Spivak, 27
Stagg, 14
Stark, 80, 82
Steinberg, 12
Stolley, 19
Stoneman, 28
Strauch-Brown, 79
Straus, 13, 14
Strueming, 7
Sullivan 29
Swan, 85

Telleger, 13
Terry, 11
Thomas, 14, 36, 27
Tierney, 89
Trikett, 14
Trivette, 33-34
Turner, 89

Valdez, 16

Wagner, 6, 78
Webster-Stratton, 28
Weigert, 36
Weitzman, 5, 79, 81
Welch, 85
Werner, 12
Whipple, 89
Whitman, 20-21
Wimbusch, 36
Winkelby, 3
Wolock, 14
Wood, 16
Wright, 15-16

Yankey, 28
Yans, 12

Zeifert, 79
Zeisemer, 18, 20